DIET FOR THE 21st CENTURY

The Complete Guide to Egg-Free Meatless Cooking

Including 100 Non-dairy Recipies

David Wright

Kim's Printers
Los Angeles

Dedicated to Srila Prabhupada

who selflessly distributed world-wide the knowledge of the
abundant spiritual and material benefits of vegetarianism.

First printing 1984, 1,000 copies
Second printing 1986, 500 copies
Third printing, 1988, 500 copies
Fourth printing, 1989, 1,000 copies

Canadian Cataloguing in Publication Data

Wright, David

Includes Index.
Bibliography:
ISBN 0-9692669 0-1

1. Vegetarian cookery. 1. Title
TX 837.W75 1986   641.5 636 C86-091522-0

PREFACE

For the benefit of all health-seeking persons, conscious of the inseperable link between a natural balanced diet and optimum health, I wish to share this rich compendium of culinary secrets gathered from twenty years of intensive exploration through the fascinating world of vegetarianism. Throughout my extensive travelling in Europe and the Orient, I've gathered what I consider to be the most flavorsome and nutritious dishes taken from the world's time-tested vegetarian traditions.

The Chinese have properly coined the dictum: "You are what you eat". We can also understand that to eat healthfully all that God provides for us in abundance is surely the key to better living. It is my sincere desire to offer this practical information about the essential culinary art of vegetarianism to all those eager to enjoy its many benefits, for the optimum well-being of body, mind and soul.

David Wright

March 15, 1987
Burnaby, B.C.

TABLE OF CONTENTS

INTRODUCTION

Vegetarianism is the way of the future. The latest statistics reveal that in North America today about 15 million people are already strict vegetarians and many more (more than 45 million) are seriously planning to eliminate meat from their diets in the near future. These figures bring no surprise when so many facts about the unhealthy consequences of meat eating, the growing land waste and the cruelty inflicted upon the animals are brought more and more to the attention of the public.

History shows that the majority of human kind has been vegetarian. The pervasive meat-centered diet rampant in recent western societies is a cultural and historical anomaly. Although unnatural and harmful, meat eating is deeply entrenched within western mores. This social conditioning, blindly followed by generation after generation of misinformed meat-eaters, is reinforced by the concerted efforts of meat producers who, aided by government grants, perpetuate the vile myth that meat is the only available source of complete protein. This conspiracy of ignorance is contradicted by the real facts about proper protein sources. Meat is actually a poor source of suitable protein, because its protein complex is not readily assimilated and causes excessive strain on our digestive sytem. Better and more concentrated protein is readily available in grains, milk products, beans, etc.

Another major obstacle to the dissemination of vegetarianism is the effect of meat on the tongue. A majority of people are still convinced that without meat, a meal is nutritionally deficient, or somewhat dull and less satisfying. But in fact, all those who have become vegetarians can testify that this feeling quickly vanishes; as the nutritional value of vegetarianism becomes a first-hand and satisfying experience, cravings for meat are replaced by disgust at the very thought of it.

Knowledge is our best weapon to overcome our conditioning to meat. Sound nutritional information is the key to achieve a proper diet and a more serene attitude towards other creatures of God. What is required is a scientific understanding of life's true nature as living spirit. Until we understand that life grows from and is maintained by the higher energy of spirit, and not dead chemicals, our ignorance and aberrant slaughtering of innocent animals will continue to soil our minds and bodies. Man's natural duty is to protect all life; a truly civilized society abhores all violence and prohibits the horrendous mass-slaughtering of innocent and valuable animals, such as the cow and bull. Surely such relentless large scale slaughter of God's creatures can only bring us violent reactions, now manifesting through increased virulent diseases such as cancer, and the horrendous mass-killing of relentless wars that continually plague mankind.

When we learn to live and eat in harmony with God's natural arrangement, we will then prosper with abundance and peace as our rewards.

Let us hope that by the turn of the century our agricultural production will serve its real purpose of properly feeding us with abundant varieties of natural wholesome foodstuffs. By then, I hope, places of horror and suffering such as today's massive slaughterhouses will have disappeared.

I feel that this present book of time-tested wholesome recipes will contribute to the public's growing interest in a meatless diet. I hope it will become a useful addition to your library and kitchen; it practically demonstrates that being a vegetarian is neither boring nor limiting, but offers you innumerable and exciting culinary choices to fully satisfy all your nutritional needs.

Pierre Gaudreau, author and religionist

WHY BE VEGETARIAN?

Let us analyse the manyfold benefits of a vegetarian diet, which amply demonstrate it to be man's natural sustenance.

NATURE'S PLAN

We can readily detect within nature's complexity the efficient workings of harmonious structures and systems. The intricate interplay of all life forms as they sustain one another reveals an inconceivably well-planned orchestration of life's dynamic forces. What is man's function within this vast network of interdependent living beings, from the microscopic amoeba to the giant whales? Our unique capacity for higher awareness allows us to reflect upon nature's complex mosaic of life and detect God's benevolent plan at work in His creation. Such heightened perception inspires us to harmonize ourselves with His perfect arrangements, by respecting and protecting all life as God-given. By God's perfect arrangements, all living beings are supplied with ample varieties of suitable foodstuffs. For man's sustenance, our Supreme Father has provided over 600 types of edible foods spread across the whole of Mother Earth. This incredible abundance and variety of vegetarian foods is surely one of nature's most irrefutable proofs that such is man's natural diet.

BETTER HEALTH THROUGH PROPER DIET

With increasing evidence of diet's critical effect on good health and longevity, more and more people are investigating this question: Is the human body better suited to a meatless diet or one that includes meat? Let us consider the biological facts. The anatomical structure of the human body, especially its teeth and digestive system, are the same as all other Herbivores (vegetarian species). The length of the human intestinal tract (12 times the body's length-the same as other Herbivores) is much longer than carniverous species (only 3 times their bodily length), which allows the slow process necessary for the fermentative bacteria to properly digest vegetarian foods. The much shorter intestinal tract of the carnivorous species, along with their stomach's very strong concentration of Hydrochloric Acid (20 times stronger than vegetarian species like man) allows them to quickly digest and eliminate rapidly decaying meat. Because the human metabolism is like that of many other herbivores (the majority of all species), we are logically drawn to conclude that vegetarian foodstuffs, the most varied and abundant foods available to man, are his natural, normal diet. That so many human societies are predominantly vegetarian is further proof to strengthen this factual conclusion.

A meat-centered diet is thus unnatural and unhealthy, as evidenced by many factual studies on the correlation between meat consumption and severe diseases. Animals destined for slaughter are breed through unnatural methods of accelerated feeding for quick growth and are thus prevented from living in their natural state and environment. These artifically bred animals (especially chickens, pigs and calves) are often disease-ridden and are fed drugs to counteract their weakened resistance to numerous deadly infections and diseases. These drugs (some of them very strong antibiotics) and many other toxins are all present in meat and eggs. Also the cholesterol content of meat and eggs is augmented through artifical feeding and breeding, further increasing the health hazards of such poor meat and eggs. It is thus of no surprise to learn that numerous deadly diseases, such as cancer and heart diseases (arterioslerosis and coronary thrombosis) are statistically linked to meat consumption. As early as 1961, the Journal of American Medical Association stated that 97% of heart disease, the cause of more than half of the deaths in the U.S.A., could be prevented by a meatless diet. Numerous other studies since then have demonstrated diseases, such as colon cancer, kidney abcesses and stones, gout and many cardio-vascular diseases, such as thrombosis and arteriosclerosis could be prevented by a meatless diet. In his Notes on the Causation of Cancer, Rollo Russell writes, "I have found of 25 nations eating flesh largely, 19 had a high cancer rate and only one had a low rate, and that of 35 nations eating little or no flesh, none had a high rate." Vegetarians, such as many Oriental people of India, Tibet, and Japan, enjoy greater health, vitality and longevity.

VARIETY FOR OPTIMUM NUTRITION

Eating many varieties of wholesome (unprocessed) foods assures us the optimum nutritional value in a meatless diet. The best, most complete protein (our body's main building block and source of energy) can be obtained by regularly eating the proper food combinations. The vital principle of protein complementality (in which different foods' yeild of usable protein are significantly increased) is achieved when foods rich in protein, such as milk products, grains and beans, are regularly eaten together. Grains, our staple foodstuff, must be taken in the same meal with milk products (or beans) to yield their full nutritional value. This proper combination of foodstuffs occurs in most meals due to obvious customary usage, such as bread and butter, cereals with milk or yogurt, rice and soya sauce, etc.

AVOIDING ECONOMIC WASTE

The economic imperative of universal vegetarianism is now amply documented. There is a horrendous waste of grain stocks in a meat-centered agricultural system. The ratio of meat per quantity of grains fed to livestock is incredibly inefficient; 97% of all grain crops are fed to animals; only 10% of this total feed is transformed into meat for consumption! The per-acre yield of usable protein is 10 to 15 times greater for grain crops (soya, rice, corn or wheat) used to feed humans than the same acreage used to fatten beef cattle. The absurdity of this agricultural waste is heightened by the fact of the growing food shortage in less productive areas of the world. Can we afford to sustain such absurd affluence when others go hungry? Rene Dumont, an agricultural economist of France's National Agricultural Institute, submitted a report to the U.N. World Food Conference (Rome 1974), showing the complete irrationality of our agricultural systems: "The over-consumption of meat by the rich means hunger for the poor. This wasteful agriculture must be changed, by the suppression of feedlots where beef are fattened on grains, and a massive reduction of beef cattle". A.H. Boerma, director of the U.N. Food and Agriculture Organization (FAO), also concluded: "If we are to bring about a real improvement in the diet of the neediest, we must aim at a greater intake of vegetable protein". We can greatly assist in vastly expanding the world food supply by adopting a meatless diet and thus help eradicate so much needless suffering for humankind. A meatless diet is not only economically efficient, but it also promotes good health, reduces stress, improves moral attitudes toward all other life, and opens new worlds of eating pleasure.

By experimenting with the many varieities of wholesome dishes presented in this book, you can discover your own favorites and help introduce others to a new and unlimited realm of healthy plesures. In these pages the author has successfully captured for you the quintessence of international meatless gastronomy in a very easy to understand presentation. Please enjoy and share its many benefits.

S pices & specialties

Spices serve a dual purpose: to add flavor and enhance the taste of other foods, and to fortify the body with their unique medicinal properties.

Anise Seed is a sweet spice which tastes like licorice. Fennel seeds, available at almost any store, can be used as a substitute.

Ajwain Seed has the fragrance of oregano, although stronger. It can be purchased at Indian stores and some large supermarkets. Oregano may be used as a replacement.

Asafoetida is obtained from the dried root resins of particular plants from the parsley family. It's a fine, powdered spice that is very strong and should be used sparingly. Asafoetida replaces onions and garlic. It's available in Indian or some Chinese specialty shops, and is sometimes sold under the name of "hing".

Bay Leaf is easily available in supermarkets or grocery stores.

Black Cumin, or black jeera, can be purchased at Indian stores. It's much stronger and different than ordinary brown cumin. Caraway seed may be substituted but the taste is not exactly the same.

Cardamom is an imported sweet spice. In Indian stores, it comes in a green or white pod with little black seeds inside. Most stores sell cardamom powder.

Cayenne is a dark red powder made from dried, hot red pepper. Cayenne is the main "hot" spice in Indian food and should be used with care. It is also very high in vitamin C and helps digestion.

Channa ka Masala is a spice mixture available in Indian stores.

Cinnamon is the inner bark of any tree that is part of the Laurel species. Most cinnamon sold in Canada is actually cinnamon cassia, a slightly bitter substitute for the real thing. Cassia is both sweet and hot. If a recipe calls for the whole stick of cinnamon, the stick should be removed before the meal is served. Cinnamon sticks may be hard to find, but cinnamon powder is readily available. One cinnamon stick equals 2.5 mL (1/2 tsp.) cinnamon powder.

Cloves are the dried flower buds from tropical evergreen trees from the myrtle family. Cloves, if used whole in Indian cooking, should be removed before eating. Powder cloves by dry roasting and grinding them.

Coriander is also known as Chinese parsley. Coriander powder is made from crushed coriander seeds. This is found in stores that sell Mexican or Chinese condiments as well as Indian stores. Grind the seeds in a pepper mill to ensure freshness. Fresh coriander leaves are far tastier than ground coriander, besides being a good source of protein and vitamin C.

Cumin, the most common spice in Indian cooking, can be bought in most stores. Prepare powdered cumin by powdering dry roasted seeds in a pepper mill.

Curry Leaves are dried or fresh sweet neem leaves. Buy this spice in Indian or specialty import stores. If you can't find it, just omit it from the recipe.

Curry Powder is a spice blend containing ground curry leaves, preferably fresh.

Fennel Seeds are readily available and can replace anise.

Fenugreek Seeds are yellow and have a slightly bitter but pleasant taste. Fenugreek will aid digestion. If not available, this spice can be omitted. To make the powder, which sometimes.replaces asafoetida, simply grind the unroasted seeds.

Garam Masala is a combination of various spices, including coriander, allspice, cloves and cumin. It's available in Indian food stores.

Ginger Powder can be purchased at most grocery stores.

Ginger Root is a tough, brown root, available in most large groceries. The powdered form is a poor substitute for the strong, pungent and refreshing flavor of fresh ginger. Ginger has a tendency to dry out when stored, but can be rehydrated by soaking in warm water. It's widely used to improve flavor and stimulate digestion. Fine chop with a cheese grater.

Kolunji Seeds have a peppery taste, a bit like oregano when heated. Buy them at Indian food stores.

Mango Powder, or Amchur powder, is available in Indian stores.

Mustard Seeds (black) are an essential part of Indian cooking. They taste different than the yellow variety, which are used for mustard powder and should not be substituted for black. The black seeds are used to saute many vegetable dishes. Buy them in Indian food stores, import stores, and some grocery stores.

Nutmeg is a strong spice to be used sparingly. Though usually sold as a powder, it's almost walnut-sized when whole.

Pepper is rarely used as a spice in Indian cooking. It's best when ground fresh from peppercorns and used in salads or yogurt dishes.

Rose Water is an aromatic liquid made from rose petals, commonly used as a flavouring for sweet dishes and yogurt.

Saffron is the golden stigma of crocus plants that are grown in India as well as in parts of Europe. It is one of the most expensive spices in the world and is used both for its colouring ability and the unique aroma it gives to dishes.

Tamarind is a fruit resembling fresh peas in the pod. When ripe, tamarind posesses a sweet and sour taste. This exotic spice is best purchased in the form of instant tamarind, found in Indian stores.

Tumeric, known as a good blood purifier, is used both for its deep yellow colour and its unique taste. It's available whole (as a root) or as a powder. The powdered form is easy to find and can be stored almost indefinitely.

OTHER ITEMS

Baking powder--use only the aluminium-free variety sold in health food stores.

Channa Dal is a type of small chickpea that has been halved.   (Chickpeas are known to many as Garbanzo beans). It's commonly available in Indian food stores. Ordinary split yellow peas are quite suitable as a substitute.

Chapati Flour is a fine, very nutritious whole wheat flour. Sold as "Atta" flour in Indian stores, it's especially useful for making chapatis, or unleavend whole wheat bread.

Chickpea Flour is delicious and high in protein. It's used for special occasions as opposed to the daily diet. Garbanzo beans are slightly different than chickpeas, and Garbanzo flour is courser. Chickpea flour, also known as besan flour, can be found at any good Indian food store.

Demerara Sugar is a very nice natural brown sugar available everywhere. Unfortunately not so common in the U.S.A.

Honey should be unpasteurized. As much as possible, it should never be cooked or baked as this deteriorates its natural qualities and nutritional value.

Molasses--use the unsulphered variety sold in health food stores.

Mund Dal is the most common and flavourful legume of the Orient, where it's used for soups or sprouting. Both yellow and green varieties can be purchased at Indian or health food stores.

Red Miso is an exotic paste available in Chinese speciality shops.

Sugar--use only raw sugar (available from health, natural, or Indian food stores or in the U. S. as turbinado sugar). A few of the reasons refined sugar is harmful is because it weakens our metabolism's mineral balance and it weakens the body, as well as its immune system.

Toor Dal is a type of bean grown in India that resembles large yellow split peas. Indian or other imported food stores usually stock this item.

Urad Dal is another Indian-grown bean. Packed with nutrition (more protein than any other legume) and flavour (it's sometimes used as a spice), urad is more expensive but less frequently used than other dals. Only Indian stores stock it.

SPECIAL INGREDIENTS

GHEE

Ghee (butter oil) imparts such a refined, irresistable flavour that it has earned the label, "liquid gold" from those experienced in Indian cuisine. Ghee is a pure, non-fattening food that will not raise cholesterol levels in the blood. To make ghee:

1. Place 5 lbs. of butter in a large, heavy pot.
2. Heat over medium high heat until butter comes to a boil, stirring occasionally.
3. Reduce heat to a very low temperature.
4. Simmer uncovered and undisturbed, until the fatty solids have collected on the bottom and a thin layer of pale golden, crusty solid has formed on the surface. This should take about three hours. Do not overcook as the flavour is spoiled and it becomes too dark.
5. When the ghee is thus properly sedimented, it will appear as a golden liquid.
6. Strain the ghee through cheesecloth. Refrigerate the solids to add to soup or vegetables, and store the ghee in a cool place. If ghee is not available, substitute cold pressed extra virgin light vegetable oil (safflower, sunflower, or seseme oil, available at health food stores). Ghee is more expensive, but tastes far better, goes farther, and never spoils. (Ghee may be boiled rapidly on the stove until separation occurs, but the taste witll be not as good).

SEASONED GHEE

To impart a subtle flavour to simple foods, season ghee as follows: for each pound of butter add 5 cm (2 in.) piece of peeled sliced ginger root, 30 mL (2 tbs.) cumin seeds, a 5 cm (2 in.) piece of tumeric root, 15 mL (1 tbs.) whole black peppercorns, or 30 mL (2 tbs.) whole cloves to the butter as soon as it melts. Seal the container, and store in a cool place.

YOGURT

390 g (3 cups) non-instant, non-fat dry milk powder
2 L (8 cups) water
125 mL (1/2 cup) yogurt

1. Whip together milk powder and water. Using a stainless steel pot, heat (uncovered) to 43C (110F).
2. Add yogurt and mix using a wire whisk.
3. If you have a gas oven with a pilot light, simply place container in the oven for about 6 hours. If you have no gas stove, place the covered container near a heat source such as a radiator for about 6 hours. If it incubates too long a white layer of whey will form on the top. Stir it in and, next time, reduce incubation time.

YOGURT CREAM CHEESE

Pour yogurt into a previously boiled, small cotton bag, and drain until yogurt is firm. This takes about 10 hours. Salt to taste and garnish as you like. Some suggested garnishings are red or green pimentos, pineapple, etc.

CURD (FRESH CHEESE)

3 L (12 cups) whole milk
90 mL (3tbs.) lemon juice or
750 mL (3 cups) yogurt (approx.) or
10 mL (2 tsp.) citric acid (approx.)

1. Bring milk to boil, stirring the bottom occasionally.
2. When the milk starts boiling, slowly add souring agent a little at a time, until milk curdles and whey is clear. (Be careful; if you add too much souring agent, the curd can spoil and not lump together sufficently).
3. When whey is clear, remove from stove and pour into a colander with a cotton cloth lining. Run cold water over the curd until it is firmer but still warm. Fold the edges of the cotton to form a packet and wring out excess water.

CURD USES AND SPICING

When wrung out, curd can be pressed with a heavy weight, cubed, put in a colander, placed in hot ghee or oil, and fried until browned. The curd can be broken into pieces and deep fried in the same way, to be put in many different sauces or vegetable preparations. Before curdling the milk you may spice it with 25 mL (5 tsp.) paprika and 15 mL (1 tbs.) oregano or your favourite spices.

3

MILK BEVERAGES

Bring 500 mL (2 cups) milk to a boil, turn off the heat, add 15 ML (1tbs.) honey or to taste. Milk, taken hot, is very relaxing, and very good for creating finer brain tissues. A cardamom pod or 1 small cinnamon stick can be added at the beginning and strained before drinking, or use powdered spice.

Mix a little water with 15 mL (1 tbs.) carob powder and whip carob into hot milk. A little extra sweetner may be added. Carob milk may also be prepared in the same way using cold milk. Add one mashed banana after milk has boiled for a delicious banana milk drink.

Boil 500 mL (2 cups) milk, then leave on low heat adding 6 sliced blanched almonds; 4 or 5 threads crushed saffron; a pinch of cloves; cinnamon and cardamom powder. Boil for approximately 5 minutes. A small cinnamon stick, 1 whole clove and 1 cardamom pod may be used instead of the powdered spices, but remember to strain out the whole spices to avoid an unpleasant surprise. For exotic cullinary taste, add 10-12 peeled and sliced pistachios while milk is boiling.

BUTTERMILK DRINK

Whip 2 parts of buttermilk with 1 part water, sweeten to taste, and pour into a glass full of finely crushed ice. If you like you can add a little lemon juice, or a few drops of rose water.

ORANGE NECTAR

375 mL (1 1/2 cups) buttermilk
375 mL (1 1/2 cups) orange juice
honey to taste

Blend all ingredients, serve chilled.

DELICIOUS NECTAR

1-375 mL (12 oz.) tin frozen orange juice with 3 tins of water
**   added**
500 mL (2 cups) yogurt
1-375 mL (12 oz.) tin frozen sweetened grape juice with 3 tins
**   of water added**

Whip all ingredients until smooth.

PINEAPPLE NECTAR

310 mL (1 1/4 cups) thick yogurt
625 mL (2 1/2 cups) water
250 mL (1 cup) pineapple juice
honey to taste

Blend all ingredients, serve chilled. For variation, use your favourite juice. For extra taste and texture, fresh berries of your choice may be blended in.

TASTY NECTAR
(Non dairy)

2-375 mL (12 oz.) tins frozen orange juice
**   dilluted with 3 tins water**
1-485 mL (15 oz.) tub frozen

Blend all ingredients.

MANGO NECTAR
(Non dairy)

1 part tinned mango pulp (available at Indian stores)
1 part orange juice
honey to taste

Blend all ingredients and serve chilled.

AVACADO NECTAR

Simply put two ripe avocados in blender and blend with enough milk to make a thick nectar, sweeten to taste.

DATE MILK SHAKE

500 mL (2 cups) whole milk
10-12 soft pitted dates
1 or 2 bananas
2.5 mL (1/2 tsp.) vanilla

Blend all ingredients, serve chilled.

CAROB AND BANANA SHAKE

1L (4 cups) whole milk
30-45 mL (2-3 tbs.) honey or to taste
1 ripened banana
45 mL (3 tbs.) carob powder
2.5 mL (1/2 tsp.) smooth cashew butter

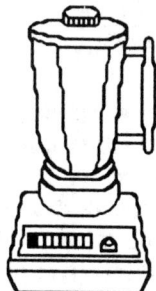

IMITATION WINE
(Non dairy)

2-375 mL (12 oz.) tins frozen sweetened grape juice
   with 6 tins of water added
750 mL (3 cups) lemon or lime juice
2-375 mL (12 oz.) tins frozen apple juice with 6 tins
   of water added
warmed honey to taste

   Whip all ingredients until blended. If concentrated juice is frozen hard, mix it in the blender with some water and blend until smooth. Chill. The same amount of bubbly mineral water may be substituted for plain water.

LEMONADE
(Non dairy)

250 mL (1 cup) fresh or bottled lemon juice
2 L (8 cups) water
warmed honey to taste

   Combine all ingredients. Serve chilled. This can be a base to make a nice nectar by adding yogurt with extra honey, orange juice or both.

FOUR FRUIT PUNCH
(Non dairy)

500 mL (2 cups) apple juice
250 mL (1 cup) cranberry juice cocktail
250 mL (1 cup) orange juice
30 mL (2 tbs.) lemon juice
5 mL (1tsp.) vanilla
250 mL (1 cup) chilled ginger ale

   Mix together fruit juices and vanilla. When ready to serve add ginger ale.

4

*E*xotic Soups

CHANNA DAL
(Non dairy)
195 g (1 cup) washed split channa dal
1.5 L (6 cups) water
1/2 tomato, washed and cubed small
2.5 mL (1//2 tsp.) turmeric
60 mL (1/4 cup) ghee or light vegetable oil
5 mL (1 tsp.) cumin seeds
5 mL (1 tsp.) black peppercorns
2.5 mL (1/2 tsp.) asafoetida
5 mL (1 tsp.) channa ka masala
7.5 mL (1/2 tbs.) sea salt
15 mL (1 tbs.) molasses

1. Combine channa beans, water, turmeric, tomato and salt in a pot and boil uncovered until the beans are soft. Add some water as needed and stir occasionally.
2. Prepare the "chaunce" in this way: Heat ghee or oil in a small frying pan until it just begins to smoke, add the cumin seeds and when browned add the peppercorns. Combine remaining powdered spices and brown lightly. You should then add the "chaunce" to the boiling water but do it very carefully as the hot spices will splatterback up. I recommend that you have the lid nearby when doing this and put it in place immediately; then add the molasses and salt. Serves 4-6

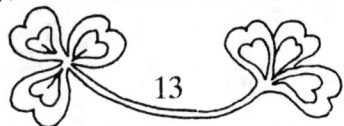

SPLIT MUNG DAL
(Non dairy)

225 g (1 cup) washed split mung beans, without skins
1.5 L (6 cups) water
2 medium tomatoes, washed and cubed
5 mL (1 tsp.) cumin powder
5 mL (1 tsp.) coriander or fenugreek powder
2.5 mL (1/2 tsp.) turmeric
15 mL (1 tbs.) ginger root cubed small
60 mL (1/4 cup) ghee or light vegetable oil
5 mL (1 tsp.) mustard seeds
5 mL (1 tsp.) curry powder
2.5 mL (1/2 tsp.) cayenne
5 mL(1 tsp.) channa ka masala
5 mL (1tsp.) oregano
10 mL (2 tsp.) molasses
12.5 mL (2 1/2 tsp.) salt

1. Combine mung beans, water, tomatoes, cumin, turmeric, coriander, and ginger in a pot and boil slowly uncovered until beans are broken down. Add water as needed and stir occasionally.
2. Prepare the "chaunce" in this way: Heat ghee or oil in small frying pan until it just begins to smoke, add mustard seeds and when they begin to pop, combine the other powdered spices and add, cooking lightly for only a few minutes. Add the spices to the boiling beans, being careful not to burn yourself as the mixture may splatter. Continue to cook for a few more minutes. Add oregano, salt and molasses. Serves 4 to 6.

URAD DAL
(Non dairy)

216 g (1 cup) washed urad dal beans
1.5 L (6 cups) water
1 tomato washed and cubed small
15mL (1tbs.) grated ginger root
60 mL (1/4 cup) ghee or light vegetable oil
5 mL (1t tsp.) mustard seeds
5 mL (1 tsp.) cumin seeds
a few curry leaves
 2.5 mL (1/2 tsp.) asafoetida
2.5 mL (/2 tsp.) turmeric
2.5 mL (1/2 tsp.) cayenne
10 mL (2 tsp.) molasses
12.5 mL (2 1/2 tsp.) salt
coriander leaves to garnish

1. Combine urad dal, water, tomato, ginger and salt in a pot and boil uncovered until beans are soft. Add water as needed and stir occasionally.
2. Prepare chaunce in much the same way as in the two preceding recipes: Heat ghee or oil in small frying pan until it just begins to smoke, add mustard seeds, when they begin to pop add cumin seeds. Brown them lightly and then add curry leaves and powdered spices again browning lightly. Add mixture to boiling beans being careful not to burn yourself as the combination of the hot mixtures can produce fireworks. Continue to cook lightly for a few minutes more. Finally add coriander and molasses. Serves 4 to 6.

MUNG-URAD DAL COMBINATION
(Non dairy)

112 g (1/2 cup) washed split mung beans
108 g (1/2 cup) washed urad dal beans
1.5 L (6 cups) water
1 tomato washed and cubed small
60 mL (1/4 cup) ghee or light vegetable oil
5 mL (1tsp.) fenugreek powder
2.5 mL (1/2 tsp.) asafoetida
2.5 mL (1/2 tsp) cumin powder
2.5 mL (1/2 tsp.) turmeric powder
5 mL (1 tsp.) coriander powder
2.5 mL (1/2 tsp.) curry powder
2.5 mL (1/2 tsp) channa ka masala
2.5 mL (1/2 tsp.) cayenne
12.5 mL (2 1/2 tsp.) molasses
coriander leaves to garnish

1. Combine the mung beans, urad dal, water, tomato and salt, in a pot and boil uncovered until the beans are soft. Remember to add water and stir occasionally.
2. Prepare the chaunce in this way: Heat the ghee or oil until it just begins to smoke; add the powdered spices and fry until lightly browned. Add to the boiling soft beans. Boil for a minute longer, turn off the heat and stir in molasses, salt, and coriander leaves. Serves 4 to 6.

TOOR DAL
(Non dairy)

200 g (1 cup) well washed toor dal beans
1.5 L (6 cups) water
2 tomatoes washed and cubed
10 mL (2 tsp.) instant tamarind
50 g (1/2 cup) untoasted unsweetened coconut
15 mL (1 tbs.) grated ginger root
60 mL (4 tbs.) ghee or light vegetable oil
15 mL (1 tbs.) kalonji seeds
5 mL (1 tsp.) curry powder
2.5 mL (1/2 tsp.) asafoetida
1.2 mL (1/4 tsp.) cayenne
10 mL (2 tsp) sea salt
10 mL (2 tsp.) molasses
coriander leaves to garnish

1. Combine the instant tamarind with a little water to form a smooth paste.
2. Combine the toor dal, water tomatoes, ginger, and coconut with the tamarind paste in pot and boil uncovered until the beans are soft. Add water as needed and stir occasionally.
3. Prepare the chaunce in this way: Heat ghee or oil in a small frying pan until it begins to smoke. Add kalonji seeds, cook briefly and add powdered spices. Brown the mixture and add to the boiling soft beans. Boil a little longer and stir in the coriander, salt and molasses. Serves 5 or 6.

RASAN

Just blend the dal and add water to make thin, if needed.

DAL DHOKALI
(Non dairy)

65 g (1/2 cup) chapati flour
30 mL (2 tbs.) ghee or oil
a pinch of salt
1.2 mL (1/4 tsp.) turmeric
1.2 mL (1/4 tsp.) cayenne
water to form a stiff dough

1. Mix together all dry ingredients and ghee then add enough water to form a stiff dough.
2. Knead well and let it sit for about half an hour.
3. Roll out the dough until it is very thin and cut into 2.5 cm.(1 in.) triangles.
4. Add the triangles to boiling toor dal and boil for about 1 hour. Remember to add water as necessary.

CURRY SAUCE

750 mL (3 cups) water
500 mL (2 cups) yogurt
25 g (1/4 cup) chickpea flour
60 mL (1/4 cup) ghee or light vegetable oil
5 mL (1 tsp.) mustard seeds
5 mL (1 tsp.) cumin seeds
6 cloves
5 mL (1 tsp.) fenugreek powder
5 mL (1 tsp.) cinnamon
5 mL (1 tsp.) cayenne
5 mL (1 tsp.) turmeric
5 mL (1 tsp.) coriander powder
10 mL (2 tsp.) sea salt
10 mL (2 tsp.) molasses

1. Whip together the water, yogurt, and chickpea flour in a thick bottomed pot over a low heat.
2. Prepare chaunce in this way: Heat ghee or oil until it just begins to smoke in a small frying pan, add mustard seeds and when they begin to pop add the cumin seeds. Brown the seeds and add all the powdered spices and brown them lightly. Add the mixture to the simmering liquid, along with cloves, and stir well.
3. Cover the pot and simmer for about half an hour until it thickens. Finally stir in molasses and salt. This is delicous eaten separetely as a soup or poured over rice.

VARIATIONS

1. Adjust the amount of water to make a thicker or thinner curry sauce.
2. Indian soup may be made by adding cubed potatoes to above curry sauce and/or chopped spinach, slightly cooked.
3. Add lots of soaked and well boiled chickpeas to above curry sauce.
4. To make it extra rich and tasty a small amount of fresh ghee can be added after cooking.

KHITCHARI
(COMPLETE MEAL IN ONE)
(Non dairy)

48 g (1/2 cup) well washed basmati rice
112 g (1/2 cup) washed split mung beans
2 medium- sized carrots scrapped and sliced thin
1 small sweet potato cubed small
1.5 L (6 cups) water
78 g (1/2 cup) cracked wheat
ginger root cubed small to taste
60 mL (1/4 cup) ghee or light vegetable oil
7.5 mL (1/2 tbs.) mustard seeds
7.5 mL (1/2 tbs.) cumin seeds
7.5 mL (1/2 tbs.) ajwain seeds
7.5 mL (1/2 tbs.) fenugreek powder
2.5 mL (1/2 tsp.) asafoetida
5 mL (1 tsp.) cayenne
20 mL (4 tsp.) salt or to taste
10 mL (2 tsp.) molasses

1. Combine rice, mung beans, carrots, potatoes, and water in large thick bottomed pot and boil over high heat stirring occasionally; remember the final consistency of this should be very much like porridge-so don't add too much water.
2. While beans, rice and vegetables are cooking, toast cracked wheat and ginger root, in a thick bottomed pan, stirring constantly, and add to preparation.
3. Prepare chaunce in this way: Heat the ghee or oil in small frying pan until it just begins to smoke, add seeds, and when they begin to pop add cumin seeds. When the seeds are lightly browned add ajwain seeds, and also brown them. Add all the powdered spices, cook lightly, then add spices to the rice/bean preparation. Stir well and continue cooking until the beans, rice and vegetables are soft and the preparation has a porridge like consistency.
4. Turn off heat and add molasses and salt. Serves 10.

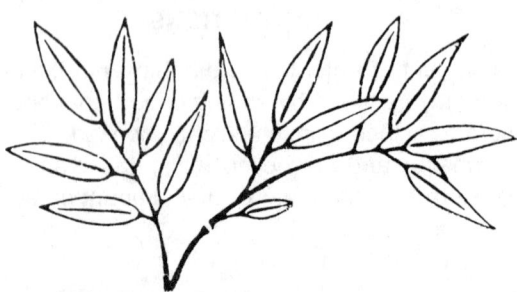

$\mathcal{M}$outh–watering Vegetables

DEEP FRIED VEGETABLES

Any of your favourite vegetables may be used to make a delicious dry vegetable preparation. Some of the most popular include potatoes, okra, cauliflower, eggplant, bitter melon, green peppers and sweet potatoes. Simply wash, peel, and cut your favourite combination, deep fry and drain well. Other steamed vegetables may be added such as peas and string beans. Spice simply with salt,cayenne, asafoetida and a few coriander leaves if you like. Use seasoned ghee with the deep fried vegetables to enjoy a culinary experience not quickly forgotten.

HOW TO PREPARE
TASTY BOILED VEGETABLES

Where I was brought up vegetables meant boiled vegetables and usually of the canned variety. It wasn't until I was older that I became aware of any other way to prepare them. Vegetables cook better if cut into bite-sized pieces; they should be boiled with a minimum of water, just enough to form a sauce when mixed with chaunced mustard and cumin seeds, cayenne and coriander. Butter, margarine or yogurt can be added, along with a little sweetener if you like. Try not to overcook - soft, but not mushy, should be the rule.

To remove 100% of surface sprays such as DDT, arsenic and cyanide, plug your sink and fill it half full of cold water. Stir in the juice of 1/2 fresh lemon and 60 mL (4 tbs.) table salt until dissolved. Soak all produce 3 or 4 minutes, swish around, and rinse under cold water.

CREAMED VEGETABLES

Steam vegetables that are to be used in a cream sauce; deep frying is not usually recommended. Some nice vegtables to steam for creamed vegetables are: broccoli, peas, potatoes, cauliflower, brussel sprouts, cabbage, carrots, corn and asparagus.

BASIC WHITE SAUCE

**125 mL (1/2 cup) salted butter
60 g (1/2 cup) unbleached flour
1 L (4 cups) whole milk
15 ml (1 tbs.) paprika
2.5 mL (1/2 tsp.) sea salt or to taste
1.2 mL (1/4 tsp.) black pepper (opp)
parsley or coriander leaves to garnish**

Melt butter in sauce pan, slowly add flour, stirring occasionally on low heat until flour is slightly browned. Gradually stir in milk along with paprika, using a wire whisk. Stir constantly until the mixture is smooth and thick and comes to a boil. To obtain a thin sauce use less butter and flour. For a thicker sauce, increase the butter and flour. Add salt and remaining spices.

VARIATIONS

1. Cream sauce - use cream instead of milk.
2. Curry sauce, use 10 mL (2 tsp.) curry powder.
3. Cheese sauce #1, add 30-60 mL (2-4 tbs.) grated medium cheddar cheese to sauce with spices, reduce amount of salt to a pinch.
4. Cheese sauce #2, use chickpea flour instead of unbleached flour, follow above recipe, reducing milk a bit.
5. Rice flour or corn flour sauce - follow same recipe as for basic white sauce, but replace unbleached flour with rice or corn flour.

CREAMY CAULIFLOWER

1 Medium cauliflower, washed and cut in bite-size flowerettes
2 L (8 cups) whole milk
Pinch of high quality saffron
ghee or light vegetable oil for deep frying
10 mL (2 tsp.) sea salt or to taste
2.5 mL (1/2 tsp.) asafoetida (or to taste)

1. Deep fry cauliflower until soft but not mushy, in medium hot ghee or oil. Drain well.
2. Add milk and saffron to a large thick bottomed pot and cook down to 500 mL (2 cups) stirring occasionally. If it starts to foam over top of pot, dip a ladle in and out of the milk to lower the foam.
3. Stir cauliflower in condensed milk along with spices and salt and stir well. Serves 2 or 3.

POTATOES, GREEN PEPPERS AND COCONUT
(Non dairy)

4 or 5 medium potatoes scrubbed and cut in 2.5 cm.
(1 in.) cubes
1 large green pepper, washed, halved, white portion removed and cubed small.
50 g (1/2 cup) medium lightly toasted coconut
60 ml (4 tbs.) ghee or light vegetable oil for frying
90 mL (6 tbs.) ghee or light vegetable oil
10 mL (2 tsp.) mustard seeds
10 mL (2 tsp.) cumin seeds
a few curry leaves
30 mL (2 tbs.) finely grated ginger root
7.5 mL (1 1/2 tsp.) cayenne or to taste
10 mL (2 tsp.) curry powder
5 mL (1 tsp.) turmeric
10 mL (2 tsp.) sea salt (or to taste)

1. Brown potatoes in frying pan with a little gheeor oil, add water to cover bottom of pan, cover and steam until soft.
2. Prepare chaunce in this way: Heat ghee or oil in thick bottomed pot until it just begins to smoke, add mustard seeds. When they begin to pop, add cumin seeds and brown lightly. Then add curry leaves and brown lightly. Then add ginger root and fry lightly. Add potatoes, green peppers and coconut with powdered spices. Fry, stirring frequently until peppers are a little soft. Turn off heat and add salt, stirring well. Serves 4.

PEAS, CARROTS AND POTATOES

4 medium potatoes scrubbed and cut in 2.5 cm (1 in. cubes)
2 medium carrots peeled and cut in1.2 cm (1/2 in.) pieces
250 mL (1 cup) peas
1 L (4 cups) half yogurt and water mixture
25 g (4 tbs.) chickpea flour unsifted
ghee or light vegetable oil for deep frying
90 mL (6 tbs.) ghee or light vegetable oil
10 mL (2 tsp.) cumin seeds
10 mL (2 tsp.) fennel seeds
2.5 mL (1/2 tsp.) asafoetida or to taste
2.5 mL (1/2 tsp.) turmeric
10 mL (2 tsp.) coriander powder
5 mL (1 tsp.) ginger powder
15 mL (1 tbs.) garam masala
15 mL (1 tbs.) sea salt or to taste
coriander leaves to garnish

1. Deep fry potatoes in hot ghee or oil until soft and browned, then drain.
2. Prepare the chaunce in this way: Heat ghee or oil in a thick bottomed pot until it just begins to smoke, add cumin and fennel seeds. When browned add asafoetida and turmeric. Brown lightly and add carrots. Stir in coriander and ginger powder, add a little water, and steam over medium heat; after five minutes, add peas and steam until carrots are soft. Stir occasionally, add water if needed.
3. Combine yogurt and water with chickpea flour, garam masala and coriander leaves and stir into hot vegetables along with potatoes and cook until thickened. Add salt. To give a creamier consistency and sharper taste use 1 L (4 cups) of yogurt instead of the yogurt and water mixture. Serves 4 to 6.

POTATOES AND YOGURT

4 or 5 medium potatoes scrubbed and cut in 2.5 cm. (1 in.) cubes
500 mL (2 cups) yogurt (opp)
ghee or light vegetable oil for deep frying
90 mL (6 tbs.) ghee or light vegetable oil
15 mL (1tbs.) curry powder
2.5 mL (1/2 tsp.) asafoetida or to taste
5 mL (1tsp.) cayenne or to taste
15 mL (1 tbs.) coriander
15 mL (1 tbs.) demerara sugar

439
on km

atoes in hot ghee or oil until soft, then drain.
ntil it just begins to smoke, add potatoes and all spices.
gh heat for a few minutes stirring constantly. Turn off heat
, sweetener and yogurt. Stir well. As a variation you can
yogurt with curd or just eliminate the yogurt.
4.

POTATOES, GREEN PEPPERS AND TOMATOES .
(Non dairy)

potatoes scrubbed and cut in 2.5 cm (1 in.) cubes
green pepper washed, cut in half, white portion
ed and cubed small.
s) tomatoes washed and blended

ghee or light vegetable oil for frying
90 ml (6 tbs.) ghee or light vegetable oil
10 mL (2 tsp.) mustard seeds
2.5 mL (1/2 tsp.) cumin seeds
2.5 mL (1/2 tsp.) fennel seeds

2.5 mL (1/2 tsp.) ajwain seeds
2.5 mL (1/2 tsp.) asafoetida or to taste
2.5 mL (1/2 tsp.) turmeric
5 mL (1 tsp.) cayenne or to taste

5 mL (1 tsp.) coriander
10 mL (2 tsp.) sea salt or to taste
30 mL (2 tbs.) demerara sugar
corainder leaves to garnish

1. Brown potatoes in frying pan with a little ghee or oil, add water to cover bottom of pan, cover and steam until soft.
2. In separate pan cook down tomatoes with all powdered spices and green pepper until thick consistency is obtained.
3. Prepare chaunce in this way: Heat ghee or oil until it just begins to smoke, add mustard seeds; when they begin to pop add cumin and fennel seeds; when they are lightly browned add ajwain seeds, cook lightly and stir in potatoes along with tomatoes. Turn off heat and stir in salt and sweetener. Garnish. Serves 4 or 5.

CHICKPEA SURPRISE
(Non dairy)

After washing well, soak chickpeas for several hours. Boil chick-peas until they are soft. Stir in your favourite spiced tomato sauce.

PLANTAIN VEGETABLE
(Non dairy)

2 large plantains, ripe enough so skin is easily removed and
cut in 1.2 cm. (1/2 in.) pieces.
1 L (4 cups) tomatoes, washed and blended
1 pineapple, cubed small
2.5 mL (1/2 tsp.) coriander
2.5 mL (1/2 tsp.) ginger powder
1.2 mL (1/4 tsp.) cinnamon
2.5 mL (1/2 tsp.) cloves
2.5 mL (1/2 tsp.) cardamom powder
1.2 mL (1/4 tsp.) nutmeg
30 mL (2 tsp.) demerara sugar
125 ml (1/2 cup butter or soft margarine
15 mL (1 tsp.) sea salt or to taste

1. Boil plantain for 5 minutes only and drain.
2. Cook down tomatoes until a thick consistency with all powdered
spices.
3. Stir in pineapple and plantain, sweetener, butter or margarine and
salt. Serves 4 to 6.

GAURANGA POTATOES

4 or 5 medium potatoes scrubbed and sliced 1.2 cm 1/2 inch
thick
500 mL (2 cups) sour cream
3 L (12 cups) water
15 mL (1 tbs.) turmeric
15 mL (1 tbs.) fenugreek powder
5 mL (1 tsp.) asafoetida or to taste
15 mL (1 tsp.) sea salt or to taste
15 mL (1 tbs.) paprika
coriander leaves or parsley to garnish

1. Boil the potatoes in water with turmeric until soft but not mushy.
2. Drain.
3. Stir fenugreek powder, asafoetida and salt into sour cream.
4. Spread potatoes evenly in a large baking pan, pour the sour cream
evenly over top.
5. Bake at 177C (350F) for about 1 hour.
6. Sprinkle paprika over top when done and garnish.
Serves 3 or 4.

ZUCCHINI, TOMATOES
AND POTATOES

(Non dairy)

5 average sized zucchini, washed and cut in half, then cut in
small french fry type pieces
4 or 5 medium potatoes scrubbed and cut in 2.5 cm. (1 in.) cubes
1 L (4 cups) tomatoes, washed and blended
150 g (1 cup) roasted chopped cashew nuts
90 mL (6 tbs.) ghee or light vegetable oil
30 mL (2 tsp.) mustard seeds
a few curry leaves
5 mL (1 tsp.) ajwain seeds
5 mL (1 tbs.) coriander powder
5 mL (1 tsp.) cayenne or to taste
15 mL (1 tbs.) curry powder
5 mL (1 tsp.) asafoetida or to taste
30 mL (2 tsp.) demerara sugar
22 mL (1 1/2 tbs.) sea salt or to taste

1. Place zucchini in pan, add water to cover bottom of pan, cover and
   steam until soft.
2. Brown potatoes in frying pan with a little ghee or oil, add water to cover
   bottom of pan, cover and steam until soft.
3. Cook down tomatoes with all powdered spices until a thick consistency.
4. Prepare chaunce in this way: Heat ghee or oil in thick bottomed pot
   until it just begins to smoke, add mustard seeds, when they begin to
   pop add curry leaves. When they are lightly browned add ajwain
   seeds, brown, then add all vegetables. Fry for a few minutes stirring
   frequently over high heat. Turn off heat and stir in sweetener, salt and
   cashews. Serves 4 to 6.

BROCCOLI VEGETABLE
(Non dairy)

**1 bunch of broccoli, washed with woody stem removed, and
cut in bite-sized pieces
1 L (4 cups) tomatoes washed and blended
90 mL (6 tbs.) ghee or light vegetable oil
10 mL (2 tsp.) dill seeds
10 mL (2 tsp.) cumin seeds
5 mL (1 tsp.) asafoetida or to taste
10 mL (2 tsp) sea salt or to taste
250 mL (1 cup) sour cream (opp)**

1. Prepare chaunce in this way: Heat ghee or oil in thick bottomed pot
   until it just begins to smoke, add dill seeds, brown sightly, and add
   cumin seeds. Brown them lightly and add asafoetida. Add vegetables, continue cooking uncovered until the broccoli is soft but not
   mushy, remembering to stir occasionally.
2. Turn off heat and stir in sour cream, if desired, and salt.
   Serves 4 to 6.

SPINACH AND POTATOES
(Non dairy)

**568 g (1 bag) spinach, washed and chopped
4 medium potatoes scrubbed and cut in 2.5 cm. (1 in.) cubes
90 mL (6 tbs.) ghee or light vegetable oil
10 mL (2 tsp.) mustard seeds
5 mL (1 tsp.) cumin seeds
5 mL (1 tsp.) asafoetida or to taste
5 mL (1 tsp.) cayenne or to taste
2.5 mL (1/2 tsp.) turmeric
10 mL (2 tsp.) sea salt or to taste
15 mL (1 tbs.) demerara sugar**

1. Brown potatoes in a little ghee or oil, add water to cover bottom of pan,
   cover and steam until soft.
2. Prepare chaunce in this way: Heat ghee or oil until it just begins to
   smoke in thick bottomed pot. Add mustard seeds, when they begin
   to pop add cumin seeds and brown lightly. Add powdered spices,
   again brown lightly then add vegetables, stirring constantly over
   medium high heat until spinach is cooked, but not mushy. Turn off
   heat and stir in salt and sweetner. As a variation you can add 250 mL
   (1 cup) of sour cream at this point. Serves 3 to 4.

SPICY CAULIFLOWER
(Non dairy)

1 medium cauliflower, washed and cut in bite-sized pieces
1 medium green pepper, washed, halved, white portion
   removed and cubed small
1L (4 cups) washed and blended tomatoes
90 mL (6 tbs.) ghee or light vegetable oil
5 mL (1 tsp.) mustard seeds
5 mL (1 tsp.) cumin seeds
a few curry leaves
5 mL (1 tsp.) ajwain seeds
5 mL (1 tsp.) channa ka masala
5 mL (1 tsp.) curry powder
2.5 mL (1/2 tsp.) turmeric
5 mL (1 tsp.) instant tamarind
15 mL (1 tbs.) demerara sugar
15 mL (1 tbs.) molasses
15 mL (1 tbs.) sea salt or to taste
a few coriander leaves to garnish

1. Cook down tomatoes with powdered spices and instant tamarind.
2. Prepare the chaunce in this way: Heat ghee or oil in a thick bottomed pot until it just begins to smoke, add mustard seeds, when they begin to pop add cumin seeds. When the seeds are lightly browned add curry leaves, and ajwain seeds. When all spices are nicely browned add cauliflower, and peppers, fry until soft over medium heat in a covered pot and stir frequently.
3. Add cooked-down tomatoes to cauliflower and peppers. Add sweeteners, salt and coriander leaves. Serves 3 or 4.

STRING BEANS
(Non dairy)

1 kg (5 cups) string beans, washed with ends cut and halved
95 g (2/3 cup) roasted unsalted peanuts
60 mL (1/4 cup) butter or soft margarine
15 mL (1 tbs.) coriander powder
45 mL (3 tbs.) lemon juice
10 mL (2 tsp.) sea salt or to taste

1. Steam string beans in colander until soft.
2. Melt butter or margarine in thick bottomed pot, add beans and coriander, fry 2 minutes, stirring constantly over high heat.
3. Turn off heat and stir in lemon juice, salt and peanuts.

OKRA CURRY

1 Kg (5 cups) okra, washed, with ends cut off and halved
250 mL (1 cup) yogurt
250 mL (1 cup) water
30 mL (2 tbs.) chickpea flour
90 mL (6 tbs.) ghee or light vegetable oil
5 mL (1 tsp.) cumin seeds
15 mL (1 tbs.) coriander powder
10 mL (2 tsp.) sea salt or to taste

1. Prepare chaunce in this way: Heat ghee or oil in thick bottomed pot until it just begins to smoke, add cumin seeds and fry until browned. Add okra and cook over medium heat stirring frequently until soft.
2. Beat together yogurt, water, chickpea flour and coriander and boil over high heat for about 2 minutes.
3. Stir liquid into cooked okra and add salt. Serves 4 to 6.

CABBAGE, POTATOES & TOMATOES
(Non dairy)

1 small green cabbage washed and shredded
4 or 5 medium potatoes cut in 2.5 cm (1 in.) cubes
60 ml (4 tbs.) gee or light vegetable oil for frying
1 L (4 cups) washed, blended tomatoes
250 mL (1 cup) water
90 mL (6 tbs.) ghee or light vegetable oil
15 mL (1 tbs.) anise seeds
5 mL (1 tsp.) turmeric
15 mL (1 tbs.) coriander powder
30 mL (2 tbs.) sea salt or to taste
5-10 mL (1-2 tsp.) garam masala
30 mL (2 tbs.) demarara sugar

1. Brown potatoes in frying pan with ghee or oil, add water to cover bottom of pan. Cover and steam until soft.
2. Cook down tomatoes until a thick consistency.
3. To prepare chaunce : Heat ghee or oil in a thick bottomed pot until it begins to smoke, add anise seeds, toast until lightly browned.
4. Add turmeric and coriander, brown lightly, then add cabbage and fried potatoes. Fry a few minutes in the spices, until everything is coated, add water, lower heat to medium, cover and cook until cabbage is soft. Add more water if necessary during cooking, but drain excess when finished.
5. Mix in sweetener, salt and garam masala, stir well. Serves 6 to 8.

OKRA AND POTATOES
(Non dairy)

4 or 5 medium potatoes, scrubbed and cut in 2.5 cm (1 in.)
cubes
455 g (2 1/2 cups) okra washed, with ends cut off and halved
ghee or light vegetable oil for deep frying
90 mL (6 tbs.) ghee or light vegetable oil
5 mL (1 tsp.) mustard seeds
5 mL (1 tsp.) cumin seeds
a few curry leaves
5 mL (1 tsp.) cayenne or to taste
5 mL (1 tsp.) curry powder
5 mL (1 tsp.) channa ka masala
2.5 mL (1/2 tsp.) asafoetida or to taste
2.5 mL (1/2 tsp.) turmeric
10 mL (2 tsp.) sea salt or to taste

1. Brown potatoes in frying pan with a little ghee or oil, add water to cover bottom of pan, cover and steam until soft.
2. Deep fry okra in hot ghee or oil and drain.
3. Prepare the chaunce in this way: Heat the ghee or oil in thick bottomed pot until it just begins to smoke, add mustard seeds, when they begin to pop add cumin seeds. Brown lightly, add curry leaves, brown lightly then add vegetables along with powdered spices. Fry over high heat for a few minutes stirring constantly, then turn off heat, add salt. Stir the okra and potatoes well. Serves 5 to 7.

SPICY EGGPLANT
(Non dairy)

1 large eggplant washed and cut in 1.2 cm. (1/2 in.) cubes
1.5 L (6 cups) washed, blended tomatoes
125 mL (1/2 cup) salted butter or soft margarine
90 mL (6 tbs.) ghee or light vegetable oil
10 mL (2 tsp.) mustard seeds
5 mL (1 tsp.) cumin seeds
a few curry leaves
5 mL (1 tsp.) urad dal beans
5 mL (1 tsp.) ajwain seeds
5 mL (1 tsp.) asafoetida or to taste
10 mL (2 tsp.) channa ka massala
10 mL (2 tsp.) curry powder
10 mL (2 tsp.) cayenne or to taste
5 mL (1 tsp.) turmeric
22 mL (1 1/2 tsp.) sea salt or to taste
15 mL (1 tbs.) demerara sugar
15 mL (1 tbs.) molasses

1. Cook down tomatoes until thick consistency is obtained.
2. Prepare the chaunce in this way: Heat ghee or oil in a thick bottomed pot until it just begins to smoke, add mustard seeds; when they begin to pop add cumin seeds, brown lightly - add curry leaves, urad dal beans and ajawin seeds. When spices are nicely browned add eggplant, butter or margarine, powdered spices and fry on medium heat with lid on, stirring occasionally. If the eggplant should stick badly to the bottom of the pot, turn off the heat, let cool and scrape the bottom. You may resume cooking until the eggplant is mushy.
3. When eggplant is cooked, turn off heat, stir in tomatoes and the remaining ingredients. Serves 4 to 6.

EGGPLANT AND POTATOES
(Non dairy)

1 large eggplant washed and cut in 1.2 cm (1/2 in.) cubes
4 or 5 medium potatoes, cut in 2.5 cm (1 in.)cubes
ghee or light vegetable oil for frying
125 mL (1/2 cup) salted butter or soft margarine
90 mL (6 tbs.) ghee or light vegetable oil
10 mL (2 tsp.) mustard seeds
10 mL (2 tsp.) cumin seeds
10 mL (2 tsp.) urad dal beans
10 mL (2 tsp.) ajwain seeds
10 mL (2 tsp.) turmeric
10 mL (2 tsp.) channa ka masala
5 mL (1 tsp.) curry powder
7.5 mL (1 1/2 tsp.) cayenne or to taste
5 mL (1 tsp.) asafoetida or to taste
15 mL (1 tbs.) sea salt or to taste
30 mL (2 tbs.) molasses

1. Brown potatoes in frying pan with a little ghee or oil, add water to cover bottom of pan, cover and steam until soft.
2. Prepare the chaunce in this way: Heat ghee or oil until it just begins to smoke, add mustard seeds and when they begin to pop add cumin seeds. When slightly browned add urad dal beans and ajwain seeds and brown lightly. Add eggplant, butter or margarine, and powdered spices, fry covered on medium heat, stir occasionally. If eggplant sticks, take it off heat, cool down, scrape and resume cooking. When eggplant is mushy turn off heat and stir in salt, molasses and potatoes. Serves 5 to 7.

EGGPLANT, SQUASH AND TOMATOES
(Non dairy)

1 med. eggplant cut in 1.2 cm (1/2 in.) cubes
1 small squash peeled and cut in 1.2 cm (1/2 in.) cubes
1 L (4 cups) tomatoes washed and blended
125 mL (1/2 cup) butter or soft margarine
30 mL (2 tbs.) coriander powder
5 mL (1 tsp.) garam masala
15 mL (1 tbs.) demerara sugar
15 ml (1 tbs.) sea salt or to taste

Melt butter or margarine, add coriander and vegetables, cook covered over medium-high heat until vegetables are mushy. Turn off heat and stir in garam masala, sugar and salt. Serves 4 to 6.

SRILA PRABHUPADA'S
ZUCCHINI PREPARATION

5 medium zucchini, cut in 2.5 cm (1 in.) pieces
250 mL (1 cup) yogurt
90 mL (6 tbs.) ghee or light vegetable oil
10 mL (2 tsp.) cumin seeds
2.5 mL (1/2 tsp.) turmeric
2.5 mL (1/2 tsp.) asafoetida or to taste
2.5 mL (1/2 tsp.) cayenne or to taste
30 mL (2 tbs.) grated ginger root
15 mL (1 tbs.) honey
15 mL (1 tbs.) lemon juice
10 mL (2 tsp.) sea salt or to taste
coriander leaves to garnish

1. Place zucchini in pan, add water to cover bottom of pan, cover and steam until soft but still firm.
2. Prepare chaunce in this way: Heat ghee or oil in a thick bottomed potuntil it just begins to smoke, add cumin seeds and fry until browned.
3. Add powdered spices and ginger. Fry briefly and stir in zucchini. Fry a minute to coat well with the spices, turn off heat and stir in remaining ingredients. Serves 3 to 4.

CAULIFLOWER AND POTATOES

4 or 5 medium potatoes, scrubbed and cut in 2.5 cm (1 in.)
cubes
1 med. cauliflower, washed and cut in bite-sized pieces
500 mL (2 cups) yogurt
90 mL (6 tbs.) ghee or light vegetable oil
5 mL (1 tsp.) turmeric
2.5 mL (1/2 tsp.) asafoetida or to taste
15 mL (1 tbs.) coriander powder
5 mL (1 tsp.) cayenne or to taste
15 mL (1 tbs.) garam masala
15 mL (1 tbs.) sea salt or to taste
15 mL (1 tbs.) demerara sugar

1. Brown potatoes in frying pan with a little ghee or oil, add water to cover bottom of pan, cover and steam until soft. Repeat the process for cauliflower.
2. Heat ghee or oil in thick bottomed pot until it just begins to smoke, add powdered spices, except garam masala, fry until fragrant and stir in vegetables. Fry, stirring frequently over high heat for 2 or 3 minutes. Turn off heat and stir in yogurt, garam masala, sweetener, and salt. Serves 4 to 6.

VEGETABLE HALAVAH
(UPMA)
(Non dairy)

4 or 5 medium potatoes, scrubbed and cut in 2.5 cm
  (1 in.) cubes
1 small green cabbage washed and shredded
750 mL (3 cups) washed, blended tomatoes
250 mL (1 cup) water
90 g (1/2 cup) cream of wheat
125 mL (1/2 cup) salted butter or soft margarine
90 mL (6 tbs.) ghee or light vegetable oil
5 mL (1 tsp.) paprika
5 mL (1 tsp.) cumin powder
2.5 mL (1/2 tsp.) asafoetida or to taste
5 mL (1 tsp.) coriander powder
2.5 mL (1/2 tsp.) cayenne or to taste
grated ginger root to taste
15 mL (1 tbs.) molasses
15 mL (1 tbs.) sea salt or to taste

1. Brown potatoes in frying pan with a little ghee or oil, add water to cover bottom of pan, cover and steam until soft.
2. Fry cream of wheat in butter or margarine until grains are golden brown. Set aside.
3. Prepare masala in this way: Heat ghee or oil in a thick bottomed pot until it just begins to smoke. Combine paprika, cumin, asafoetida, coriander and cayenne and briefly toast, until fragrant, add ginger root and fry until lightly browned. Add cabbage, stirring constantly until well coated with spices. Add a little water, cover and steam until soft over medium heat, add more water if needed.
4. Combine all ingredients. Cook down until thick. Serves 3 to 4.

6

Fried Treats

PAKORAS

Pakoras are a very popular snack in India. They are simply vegetables dipped in a thin batter and deep fried. Almost any vegetable can be used.

STANDARD PAKORA BATTER
(Non dairy)

300 g (3 cups) chickpea flour or 240 g (2 cups)
  unbleached flour and 100 g (1 cup) chickpea flour
15 mL (1 tbs.) coriander powder
7.5 mL (1/2 tbs.) turmeric
15 mL (1 tbs.) kulunji seeds
5 mL (1 tsp.) cayenne or to taste
22 mL (4 1/2 tsp.) sea salt or to taste
500 mL (2 cups) water (approx.) or whey, (if whey, reduce salt
  by 1/2) or yogurt mixed with a little water
Your favorite vegetables, cut into bite-sized pieces.
  (Some of the best vegetables are cauliflower, carrots or
  potatoes, zucchini cut in long strips or sweet potatoes)

1. Combine all dry ingredients and add liquid to make a smooth batter.
2. Heat ghee or light vegetable oil until it is hot but not smoking.
3. Dip your favourite vegetable in batter and deep fry until vegetable is cooked and batter is golden brown. To give the batter an interesting taste, let it sit in a warm place overnight and allow it to lightly ferment.

   Prepare any style pakoras and add to maha panir wada sauce, (pg. 38). (pakoras should be on the small side). Add roasted cashews to taste. You may also add small pakoras to your favorite wet vegetable preparation. Pakoras blend well with many types of chutney, raita, or plain yogurt. They can also be served as an appetizer, side dish, or by themselves as a snack. They are very tasty dipped in a thick tomato sauce.

NON-GRAIN PAKORA BATTER
(Non dairy)

450 g (3 cups) buckwheat flour
7.5 mL (1/2 tbs.) turmeric
22 mL (4 1/2 tsp.) sea salt or to taste
15 mL (1 tbs.) sambar or curry powder
500 mL (2 cups) water (approx.)
Any of your favourite vegetables

1. Mix all dry ingredients and add water to form a thin batter.
2. Prepare as with regular pakoras.

SUPER PAKORAS

Follow any pakora batter recipe. Fold kneaded curd (see page 8) around vegetable piece. Dip in batter and fry as usual.

RICE PAKORAS

Follow plain rice recipe (see index) adding 5 mL (1 tsp.) asafoetida, 5 mL (1 tsp.) sambar or curry powder, 5 mL (1 tsp.) garam masala to boiling water before cooking rice. Cool, form into balls. If hard to form, use a little rice flour and water to bind. Deep fry as for regular pakoras using your favourite batter, but reduce salt by half.

CURD PAKORAS

Curdle 4L (1 gal.) of milk,   (see method for curd preparation on page 8), press, and cut into bite-sized cubes. Dip in favorite pakora batter and fry as usual. You can also knead and spice the curd as for curd burgers, (see index), form into discs and dip and fry as usual. Only use half as much salt in pakora batter.

EGGPLANT PAKORAS ON GRILL
(Non dairy)

300 g (3 cups) chickpea flour
7.5 mL (1/2 tbs.) turmeric
22 mL (4 1/2 tsp.) sea salt
500 mL (2 cups) water (approx.)
1 medium eggplant cut in four lengthwise and sliced in .64cm.
   (1/4 in.) pieces
ghee or light vegetable oil

1. Combine all dry ingredients, add water to form a thin batter.
2. Heat grill or large cast iron frying pan to medium high heat.
3. Apply lots of ghee or oil to the surface, dip eggplant in batter, fry on grill until golden brown on each side and soft inside. Add more ghee or oil as needed.

CURD BURGERS

One batch of curd, pressed and kneaded (see pg. 8).
7.5 mL (1/2 tbs.) sea salt
15 mL (1 tbs.) curry powder
cayenne to taste
2.5 mL (1/2 tsp.) asafoetida or to taste
molasses to taste
ghee or light vegetable oil for deep frying

1. Knead all spices very well into the curd.
2. Press with your palms into small discs and drop into medium hot ghee or oil. Fry both sides until golden brown and swollen. Add to your favourite vegetable preparation, or place in a bun, and garnish with tomatoes, lettuce and alfalfa sprouts.

STUFFED EGGPLANT
(Non dairy)

200 g (2 cups) chickpea flour
10 mL (2 tsp.) garam masala
12.5 mL (2 1/2 tsp.) sea salt
60 mL (1/4 cup) ghee or light vegetable oil
5 mL (1 tsp.) asafoetida
180 mL (3/4 cup) water (aprox.)
1 medium eggplant
untoasted coconut or coriander leaves to garnish

1. Mix dry ingredients well with ghee or oil and add water to form a thick batter.
2. Cut ends off eggplant, cut in half lengthwise and peel. Cut eggplant from bottom lengthwise in .32 cm (1/8 in.) strips. Reassemble eggplant spreading batter evenly between layers.
3. Finally cut each half into 3 pieces crosswise.
4. Deep fry pieces in medium high ghee or oil until a knife can be passed easily through each one and they are golden brown. Drain and garnish generously.

LIGHT STEAMED CAKES (IDLI)
(Non dairy)

Before attempting this preparation be sure you have an "idli maker". They can be purchased at large Indian food stores. If no idli maker is available you can settle for an egg poacher. Idliss are very tasty with coconut chutney, coriander chutney or rasam.

160 g (1 cup) rice flour
126 g (1 cup) urad dal flour
buttermilk
1.2 mL (1/6 tsp.) baking powder
sea salt to taste
finely chopped coriander leaves

1. Combine rice flour and urad dal flour and add buttermilk to form a thick batter. For every 250 mL (1 cup) batter add 1.2 mL (1/4 tsp.) salt and coriander leaves to taste.
2. Cover batter and let sit 24 hours to ferment. Then stir in baking soda. Put ghee or oil inside poacher or idli maker, fill containers 3/4 full.
3. Cover tightly, boil for 10 minutes until a rubbery, dry consistency is obtained. Serve warm.

DEEP FRIED CURD PATTIES IN TOMATO SAUCE (MAHA PANIR WADA)

4 L (16 cups) milk curdled, pressed, and kneaded (see page 8)
a few coriander leaves
10 mL (2 tsp.) curry powder
5 mL (1 tsp.) asafoetida
7.5 mL (1/2 tbs.) sea salt
cayenne to taste
15 mL (1 tbs.) molasses

1. Thoroughly knead spices into curd and form into about 25 patties.
2. Deep fry in medium hot ghee or oil until golden brown and cooked through.

SAUCE FOR CURD PATTIES
(Non dairy)

2 L (8 cups) tomatoes washed and blended
1 large green pepper, washed, halved, white portion
**   removed and cubed small**

60 mL (4 tbs.) ghee or light vegetable oil
15 mL (1 tbs.) cumin seeds
15 mL (1 tbs.) ajwain seeds
5 mL (1 tsp.) cayenne or to taste
15 mL (1 tbs.) curry powder
5 mL (1 tsp.) turmeric
5 mL (1 tsp.) asafoetida or to taste
30 mL (2 tbs.) lemon juice
15 mL (1 tbs.) molasses
15 mL (1 tbs.) sea salt or to taste
a few coriander leaves to garnish

1. Prepare the chaunce in this way: Heat ghee or oil in a thick bottomed pot until it just begins to smoke. Add cumin seeds. When lightly browned add ajwain seeds. When fried lightly and ghee or oil is still very hot add vegetables, cayenne, curry powder, turmeric and asafoetida.
2. Cook sauce until it is smooth and has thickened.
3. After sauce is thickened stir in lemon juice, molasses, salt, coriander leaves and curd patties.

BEANS GROUND AND DEEP FRIED
(BARRA)
(Non dairy)

450 g (2 cups) washed split mung beans soaked about 6 hours
 (other beans may be used)
urad dal flour or chickpea flour to thicken
cayenne
cumin powder
fenugreek powder
baking soda
sea salt
curry powder
ghee or light vegetable oil for deep frying

1. Blend mung dal beans using the water they were soaked in, using as little water as possible to form a thick batter.
2. For every 750 mL (3 cups) thick batter stir in 3.6 mL (3/4 tsp.) salt, and 7.5 mL (1/2 tbs.) powdered spices, except cayenne (which you should add to taste) and 1/4 tsp. of baking soda. If the batter won't hold shape, add flour to thicken.
3. Using a teaspoon, scoop up batter and slide off spoon (using finger) into medium hot ghee or oil. Repeat until the top of the ghee or oil is covered by these little balls. Fry until browned outside and spongy inside. If they are to be placed in spiced yogurt, soak first in very hot water for one minute, otherwise, simply add to your favourite sauce or vegetable dish. A great meat replacer.

YOGURT SAUCE

30 mL (2 tbs.) sea salt, mixed in 1 L (4 cups) yogurt
cayenne to taste
cumin powder to taste
asafoetida to taste
demerara sugar to taste
a little molasses or
a litte pani pura masala (available at Indian stroes)
a few coriander leaves to garnish

Barras are always a nice addition to vegetable preparations, soup and curry sauces, and very tasty in curd patty sauce.

Combine yogurt with all other ingredients until the spices are well mixed. If you prefer, the yogurt sauce need not be spiced; just add some melted butter to the yogurt.

BARRA VARIATIONS

Soak overnight equal amounts of urad dal beans and mung beans; or urad dal beans and chick peas; or urad dal beans and rice. Prepare and spice as for barra.

BARRA SPONGE BALLS
(Non dairy)

126 g (1 cup) urad dal flour
120 g (1 cup) unbleached flour

Prepare a thick batter with both flours combined, spice and prepare as for barra. If adding to yogurt, dip in hot water first.

LIGHT PANCAKES

(DOSA PANKCAKES)
(Non dairy)

145 g (2/3 cup) urad dal beans soaked overnight
130 g ((1 1/2 cups) basmati rice soaked overnight
sea salt
ghee or light vegetable oil

1. Blend beans and rice as for barra. The batter should be a consistency suitable for pancakes. For every 250 mL (1 cup) batter add 1.2 mL (1/4 tsp.) salt.
2. Cover batter and let sit in a warm spot to ferment for 24 hours.
3. Heat grill or frying pan to medium high temperature, and fry dosas as you would regular pancakes (see index), but very thin. Use approximately 125 mL (1/2 cup) batter for each pancake. Serve with coconut chutney.

VEGETABLE PANCAKES #1
(PUDLA)
(Non dairy)

1 Medium cauliflower, washed and grated
500 mL (2 cups) washed and cubed tomatoes
100 g (1 cup) chickpea flour
15 mL (1 tbs.) cumin seeds
10 mL (2 tsp.) curry powder
30 mL (2 tbs.) finely chopped ginger root
10 mL (2 tsp.) sea salt
ghee or light vegetable oil

1. Heat grill to a medium high temperature.
2. Combine cauliflower, tomatoes and chickpea flour.
3. Dry roast cumin seeds in a small cast iron frying pan and stir into other ingredients along with curry powder, ginger and salt.
4. Spread some ghee or oil on grill and scoop out batter 125 mL (1/2 cup) at a time. Spread to a pancake thickness and fry one side until dark brown with a few black spots. Turn over and put a little ghee or oil on top of pudla and fry other side until it is well browned. Serve with yogurt, sour cream or chutney.

VEGETABLE PANCAKE #2
(PUDHA)

568 g (1 bag) spinach, washed and finely chopped
200 g (2 cups) chickpea flour
65 g (1/2 cup) whole wheat flour
5 mL (1 tsp.) turmeric
ghee or light vegetable oil
15 mL (1 tbs.) finely chopped fresh green chillies
15 mL (1 tbs.) sea salt or to taste
250 mL (1 cup) yogurt
250 mL (1 cup) water
10 mL (2 tsp.) molasses (optional)

1. Heat grill to medium-high temperature.
2. Thoroughly mix the chickpea flour, whole wheat flour, turmeric, chillies and salt.
3. Mix together yogurt and water and mix it into the flour and spice mixture. Molasses may be added at this point if a sweetner is desired.
4. Stir in spinach and mix thoroughly. Scoop the mixture out by 125 mL (1/2 cup) measurements on to a greased hot grill.
5. Spread out very thinly (at least 15 cm (6 in.) across) so that the middle cooks well. Fry both sides until dark brown with a couple of black spots. Serve with a chutney of your choice.

KOFTA BALLS
(Non dairy)

50 mL (2 cups) grated, washed potatoes
500 mL (2 cups) grated, washed cauliflower
100 g (1 cup) chickpea flour
10 mL (2 tsp.) asafoetida
10 mL (2 tsp.) turmeric
20 mL (4 tsp.) coriander powder
15 mL (1 tbs.) sea salt or to taste
ghee or light vegetable oil for deep frying

1. Heat ghee or oil so that it is not quite smoking.
2. Squeeze all water out of potatoes and combine all ingredients.
3. Form into 3.7 cm (1 1/2 in.) balls and drop into medium hot ghee or oil. Don't let mixture sit around as it will get too wet and will   be hard to form into balls. If this should happen add a little more chickpea flour.
4. Fry the balls in ghee or oil until dark brown in color and cooked all the way through. Put these tasty treats in any wet vegetable preparation or sauce you like. Serves 4 to 6.

SAMOSAS
DOUGH
(Non dairy)
240 g (2 cups) unbleached flour
60 mL (4 tbs.) firm salted butter or margarine
90 mL (6 tbs.) cold water (approx.)

Cut butter or margarine into flour until evenly dispersed. Add water to form a stiff "puri-type" dough (see pg. 48). Knead about 5 minutes and cover with a damp cloth. Let sit for half an hour.

FILLING
1 medium cauliflower, washed and grated finely with an equal amount of frozen peas.
125 mL (1/2 cup) ghee or light vegetable oil
10 mL (2 tsp.) sea salt
5 mL (1 tsp.) cinnamon
5 mL (1 tsp.) cloves
5 mL (1 tsp.) cayenne
2.5 mL (1/2 tsp.) nutmeg
2.5 mL (1/2 tsp.) coriander powder
2.5 mL (1/2 tsp.) cumin powder
2.5 mL (1/2 tsp.) asafoetida
2.5 mL (1/2 tsp.) ginger powder
ghee or light vegetable oil

1. Heat ghee or oil in a large, thick bottomed pot until it begins to smoke. Add vegetables with other ingredients and stir occasionally over medium heat. Cook until cauliflower is soft and darker in color, then mash everything to a paste. Cook a little longer on low heat.
2. Heat ghee or oil for deep frying to medium temperature.
3. Divide dough into 12 pieces and roll out in 5 in. circles. Place 30 mL (2 tbs.) filling in centre, wet edges and fold dough over, pressing the edges together. Pinch the edges of the semi-circular samosas and fold them over to make a series of seven or eight folds. Make sure they are well sealed to avoid the filling bursting the pastry shell during the deep frying.
4. Fry the samosas until they turn a light golden brown.

Samosas may be made with an equal amount of grated potato and cauliflower. Be sure to remove all excess water. You may stuff samosas with maha panir wada curd as described on pg. 38.

DAL KACHORIES: Prepare dough using whole wheat puri recipe adding 2.5 mL (1/2 tsp.) baking powder (see pg.48). Roll dough out as for samosas (but in 16 parts). Place 30 mL (2 tbs.) barra (pg.39) in middle, fold over and seal. Cook like samosas.

$\mathcal{E}$ astern
Breads

CHAPATIS
(Non dairy)

Chapatis are very nutritious and rich in fiber, vitamins B and E, protein, iron, unsaturated fats and carbohydrates. Like all whole wheat breads, chapatis also contain phytic acid, a chemical that regulates the amount of calcium and other minerals absorbed by the body.

**195 g (1 1/2 cup) chapati flour purchased at Indian stores
(Atta flour) or 1/2 whole wheat, 1/2 unbleached flour
5 mL (1 tsp.) asafoetida (opt.)
2.5 mL (1/2 tsp.) sea salt (opt.)
180 mL (3/4 cup) warm water (approx.) or curds and whey
60 mL (1/4 cup) melted butter or soft margarine for buttering
chapatis**

1. Mix together flour, salt and asafoetida. Add water to form a slightly sticky dough and knead for about 5 minutes until a smooth and soft dough is achieved.
2. Gather dough into a compact ball, place in a bowl. Rub the surface with water until a thin film is formed, and drape with damp towel. Allow the dough to sit for 1 hour at room temperature. If the dough is well covered it can sit for 6 to 8 hours while the water and gluten form and elastic consistency.

CHAPATI COOKING EQUIPMENT

flat surface near stove
flat iron griddle
stove burners
cake rack (needed only if using electric heat)
a pair of tongs
a rolling pin
a cake tin or pie tin lined with a thick clean kitchen towel
(needed if serving chapatis later)
pastry brush or teaspoon

1. Preheat griddle to medium high temperature.
2. Roll dough into balls, and coat each one with a little flour then drape balls with a damp cloth.
3. Take the balls and flatten into a patty. Roll patties out as thin and as round as possible in as little flour as possible to approximately 18cm (7 in.) in diameter. Do not stack on top of each other as they will stick together.
4. Lift up and slap off any excess flour, put on preheated griddle, and cook until you see small white blisters appear all over dough after about 30 seconds. Turn the chapatis over and cook other side until surface blisters with air pockets, this should take about 20 seconds.
5. Lift chapati off griddle and carefully place directly on a medium high gas flame or a cake rack placed over an electric burner set to high. Almost immediately the chapati should swell, fill with hot steam and puff up. Using tongs turn chapati over, then toast it until puffed surface is marked with tiny brown and black spots.
6. Remove chapati from heat and slap out hot air so chapati collapses. Brush one side with melted butter, ghee or margarine.
7. If you don't plan to serve chapatis one after another right off the stove place each cooked chapati between the folds of a towel in cake pan.
8. It is important that chapatis have breathing space, so don't cover them so tightly that they become soggy from the steam inside them. Roll one chapati as the other is cooking on the grill.

VARIATIONS

1. Instead of water, use blended tomatoes and add oregano.
2. Use potato flour instead of regular flour, although the consistency of dough and cooked texture will be quite different.

DAMODAR ROLL

125 g (1 1/4 cups) dried chickpeas soaked overnight
     (weighed or measured before soaking)
3 L (3 quarts) whole milk curdled and pressed (see pg. 8)
125 mL (1/2 cup) salted butter
10 mL (2 tsp.) curry powder
2.5 mL (1/2 tsp.) cayenne or to taste
2.5 mL (1/2 tsp.) asafoetida
2.5 mL (1/2 tsp.) turmeric
5 mL (1 tsp.) sea salt or to taste
alfalfa sprouts

1. Boil the chickpeas until they are soft. Drain, and if you are planning to make dal save this water.
2. Melt butter in a large cast iron frying pan and add everything but salt and alfalfa sprouts.
3. Fry curd and chickpeas over a medium heat until spices are nicely toasted and curd is softened.
4. Put filling at one end of a chapati with sprouts and salt on top and roll up.

CRISPY FLAKY FRIED ROUNDS
(PAROTHAS)
(Non dairy)
EQUIPMENT NEEDED

flat surface near stove
flat iron griddle
pastry brush
pair of tongs
rolling pin
one batch chapati dough
melted butter, ghee or oil

1. Follow steps 1-3 in the chapati recipe on page 45. Brush the top of each round with ghee, margarine or butter, fold in half, seal edges, and repeat again, giving a triangular shape.
2. Carefully roll out parothas to a diameter of 18 cm (7 in.) trying to get as round as possible. If it tends to stick rub a little ghee on to the rolling pin.
3. Place 2 or 3 on a hot, well greased grill, brush top with melted butter ghee or oil fry about 15 seconds, turn over, and repeat until the parothas are crisp with a number of dark brown spots and an overall light brown hue.

STUFFED PAROTHAS

Use the same equipment as for plain parothas and follow steps 1-3 in chapati recipe on page 45 except roll out to approximately 15 cm (6 in.) diameter.

RADISH OR CAULIFLOWER STUFFING
(Non dairy)

180 mL (3/4 cup) washed grated white radishes, with water squeezed out, or grated cauliflower
22 mL (1 1/2 tbs.) fresh grated ginger root
2.5 mL (1/2 tsp.) sea salt
1.2 mL (1/4 tsp.) cayenne
1 fresh green chilli chopped small

1. Place an equal amount of stuffing on each round, spread out evenly to within 2.5 cm (1 in) of the edge. Wet edge of round, place plain round on top and very carefully seal the edges. Roll out to about 20 cm (8 in) wide being careful to grease the rolling pin if it sticks, so as not to tear the dough.
2. Grease grill well and place a couple of parothas on grill brushing top with ghee or oil while frying. Turn frequently, adding ghee or oil after every turn, until done.

CRISPY FRIED ROUNDS
(Non dairy)

390 g (3 cups) chapati flour or 1/2 whole wheat,1/2 unbleached
   flour
2.5 mL (1/2 tsp.) sea salt
30 mL (2 tbs.) peanut oil or ghee
180 mL (3/4 cup) water (approx.)
melted butter or ghee or peanut oil

1. Combine together dry ingredients and mix in oil or ghee. Add water
   gradually to form a stiff dough and knead for about five minutes.
2. Heat grill to medium high temperature.
3. Grease the table top and rolling pin. Roll the dough into 12 balls, and
   then roll out balls evenly to approx. 14 cm (5 1/2 in.) circles.
4. Grease the grill well and place a few rounds on the grill. Fry about 1
   1/2 minutes on each side pressing down with a spatula to prevent from
   puffing. Continue turning and frying until crispy.

PURIS

Puris are a delicate light bread that are usually served on a special
occasion. The dough is similar to chapati dough, the difference being
that puris are deep fried in ghee or oil until they puff up like a balloon.

WHOLE WHEAT PURIS
(Non dairy)

260 g (2 cups) chapati flour or 1/2 whole wheat and
   1/2 un bleached flour
125 mL (1/2 cup) salted firm butter or margarine
60 mL (4 tbs.) cold water (approx.)
ghee or light vegetable oil for deep frying

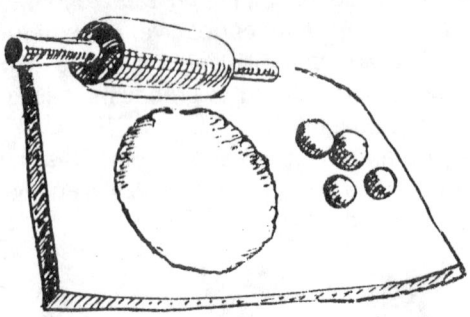

1. Cut the butter or margarine into flour with a pastry cutter, until it is evenly dispersed throughout the flour.
2. Gradually add water to form a stiff dough. This dough must not be sticky. It must be smooth and elastic. Knead for 5 minutes.
3. Let covered dough sit for half an hour.
4. Rub a little ghee or oil on the table and rolling pin. Divide the dough into 22 equal portions, roll into balls and flatten.
5. Roll out puris as round as possible to a bit under 12.7 cm (5 in.) in diameter. This procedure will take some practice to obtain the required results. If the rounds are too thin they will not puff up and if too thick they will be doughy instead of flaky.
6. When the ghee or oil is just beginning to smoke put a couple of puris in. Splash ghee on top with a large slotted spoon. When fully puffed up and the underside is browned, turn over and cook until other side is browned. Remove and drain. The finished product should be crispy, light and flaky.

VARIATIONS

1. Add 30 mL (2 tbs.) molasses to flour with the butter, mix well.
2. Masala puris: Add 10 mL (2 tsp.) asafoetida, 10 mL (2 tsp.) garam masala. Mix well with flour.
3. Add 10 mL (2 tsp.) baking powder to flour, roll out thicker and cut in sticks.
4. Instead of water use blended tomatoes with a little salt, oregano and coriander. Or instead of whole wheat flour use potato flour with a little salt and asafoetida.
5. Extra light: 260 g (2 cups) chapati flour, 60 g (1/2 cup) unbleached flour, 125 mL (1/2 cup) cold butte or margarine, 125 mL (1/2 cup) cold water.(aprox)
6. White flour puris: Use unbleached flour instead of chapati flour and the same amount of butter or margarine. Make sure the dough is good and stiff. Use less water and roll thinner than whole wheat puris. Roll in 22 balls, a bit under 15 cm (6 in.) in diameter.
7. Add 30 mL (2 tbs.) raw sugar to dough with 15 mL (1 tbs.) cinnamon.
8. Prepare sweetened carob whipping cream and with a piping bag inject the mixture into a fully puffed up puri.
9. Top the puris with a combination of honey and roasted almonds or cashews.
10. Put the cooked down fruit of your choice on one end, then roll up the puris.

BREAD STICKS

**520 g (4 cups) chapati flour or 1/2 whole wheat and
  1/2 unbleached flour
7.5 mL (1/2 tbs.) sea salt
10 mL (2 tsp.) caraway seeds
20 mL (4 tsp.) baking powder
5 mL (1 tsp.) baking soda
30 mL (2 tbs.) fresh ghee
60 mL (4 tbs.) molasses or to taste
250 mL (1 cup) whey or buttermilk
250 mL (1 cup) water
fresh ghee or light vegetable oil for deep frying**

1. Combine all dry ingredients. Combine ghee, molasses and butter-milk. Mix the two.
2. Add enough water to make a very wet sticky dough and knead dough 5 minutes.
3. Cover the dough in a bowl and let stand for about half an hour.
4. Grease rolling pin and table. Roll out .63 cm (1/4 in.) thick and cut in 7.6 cm (3in.) x 2.5 cm(1 in.) sticks.
5. Heat the ghee or oil to medium heat. Experiment with one stick to see if the temperature is right. If the ghee or oil is too hot it will not cook inside; if it's too cool it will absorb too much ghee. When sticks go in they should expand and just begin to crack after a short time. When this has happened and they are browned a little, take them out. Be very careful not to overcook; they should be soft inside but not doughy. Makes about 30 bread sticks.

ice
Rice

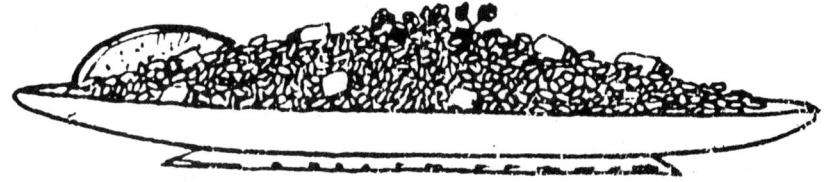

PLAIN RICE
(Non dairy)
190 g (2 cups) well washed basmati rice
750 mL (4 cups) water
75 mL (1/3 cup) butter (approx.) or light vegetable oil
7.5 mL (1/2 tbs.) sea salt

1. Add water, butter or oil and salt to a large pot with a tight fitting lid and bring to a boil. Then add rice, stir rice from bottom a couple of times as water heats.
2. When the water starts to boil cover tightly, reduce the heat to very low and steam for approximately 20 minutes.
3. After 20 minutes remove pot from stove and let sit at least 20 minutes. Gradually scrape rice bit by bit from the top into a serving bowl. This separates the grains. If the rice is still hard, next time steam over a little higher heat. If cooking more than 380 grms (4 cups) of rice add 50 % more water than rice. Serves 6.

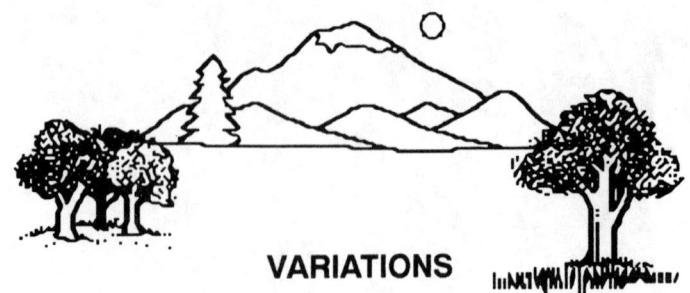

VARIATIONS

1. Sprinkle a little black pepper over the top after cooking.
2. Before rice comes to the boil stir in 15 mL (1 tbs.)curry powder, corriander powder, or dry powered spices that suit you.
3. 250 mL (1 cup) fresh peas and or 250 mL (1 cup) roasted chopped cashews or almonds may be stirred in after cooking. Do not over stir as the rice may become mushy.
4. Deep fry any amount of your favorite vegetable such as carrots, cauliflower or eggplant and stir in after cooking. Mix and match with any of the above combinations or invent your own.
5. Prepare apulau by combining the rice with herbs, spices, nuts, raisins, cheese and vegetables in a combination to suit your taste.
6. Prepare curd as on pg. 8, press, cube small, deep fry until golden. Mix in the rice.
7. Squeeze the juice of 3 or 4 lemons onto cooked rice.
8. Omit butter oroil and stir in the same amount of ghee after cooking.

YOGURT RICE

190 g (2 cups) well washed basmati or regular rice
500 mL (2 cups) yogurt
60 mL (4 tbs.) ghee or light vegetable oil
10 mL (2 tsp.) mustard seeds
5 mL (1 tsp.) asafoetida or to taste
5 mL (1 tsp.) cayenne or to taste

1. Prepare rice as on previous page.
2. Combine the yogurt and rice.
3. To prepare chaunce, heat ghee or oil until it just begins to smoke. Add mustard seeds. When they have almost finished popping, add powdered spices. Fry briefly, then, with a spatula, scrape the spices and stir into the yogurt rice. Serves 8.

SWEET YOGURT RICE

Follow yogurt rice recipe omitting step 3.
Stir in 125 mL (1/2 cup) honey, 130 g (1 cup) raisins.

Instead of raisins you may add your favorite nuts, pieces of apple, bananas, papaya, pineapple, mango, or strawberries. This is best served well chilled. Serves 8 to 10.

BHAKTIVEDANTA RICE

500 mL (2 cups) whipping cream
finely chopped (non-citrus) fruit to taste
nutmeg or cardamom to taste
48 g (1/2 cup) well washed basmati rice
honey to taste

1. Boil the rice until soft, put in a strainer and run cold water over it until all the starch is removed and the rice is fluffy. Drain well.
2. Whip the cream, combine with the rice and other ingredients and served chilled. Serves 4.

GOVINDA'S SURPRISE

1. Prepare rice as for Bhaktivedanta Rice.
2. Prepare a fruit salad equalling the amount of rice, peeling all fruit and avoiding citrus fruits and melons.
3. Combine the fruit salad and rice with yogurt. Sweeten to taste. Serves 8.

BROWN RICE
(Non dairy)

Prepare brown rice as for plain rice recipe on page 51. Instead of cooking 20 minutes, cook for 1 hour, turn off heat and steam for 5 minutes before fluffing. Don't decrease amount of water when more than 390 gms. (4 cups) rice used.

RICE SUBSTITUTE
(Non dairy)

130 g (1 cup) tapioca (available at Indian stores)
4 medium potatoes scrubbed and cut in .63 cm (1/4 in.)
    pieces
ghee or light vegetable oil for deep frying
2 medium tomatoes washed and cubed small
75 g (1/2 cup) unsalted roasted peanuts
60 mL (1/4 cup) ghee or light vegetable oil
7.5 mL (1/2 tbs.) mustard seeds
7.5 mL (1/2 tbs.) cumin seeds
7.5 mL (1/2 tbs.) coriander powder
7.5 mL (1/2 tbs.) fenugreek powder
2.5 mL (1/2 tsp.) turmeric
15 mL (1/2 tbs.) finely chopped green chillies
7.5 mL (1/2 tbs.) sea salt
coriander leaves to garnish

1. Soak the tapioca in cold water until clear, then drain.
2. Deep fry the potatoes in hot ghee or oil until brown and soft.
3. Combine the potatoes, tomatoes, nuts, soaked tapioca, salt, chilies and coriander leaves.
4. Prepare chaunce in this way: Heat ghee or oil until it just begins to smoke in a small frying pan. Add mustard seeds and whenthey begin to pop add cumin seeds. Brown the mixture and add all the other powdered spices. Toast lightly and then add to tap ioca preparation, scraping all spices off the pan with a rubber spatula. Fry everything together over high heat for a few minutes stirring often. Serves 6.

9

C ondiments

Chutney is similar to mustard, relish and catsup. It stimulates the appetite and adds zest and flavor to the meal. A chutney should be served in small portions only, as a side dish; one teaspoon is an average serving.

Another type of chutney is the pickle. Pickles differ from the daily or fresh chutney as they are prepared to last for a long time. Pickles are also referred to as preserved chutneys.

Raitas usually consist of a vegetable or fruit prepared with yogurt, salt and mustard seeds. They are similar to salads and are very simple to prepare. Flavorsome and cooling, they are served with the main meal as a refreshing accompaniment to hotter dishes. Sour cream may be substituted for yogurt.

BANANA CHUTNEY
(Non dairy)

3 medium bananas, mashed
30 mL (2 tbs.) honey
60 mL (4 tbs.) lemon juice
5 mL (1 tsp.) nutmeg or cardamom powder
60 mL (4 tbs.) salted butter or soft margarine

Combine all ingredients, except lemon juice, and cook over medium heat stirring constantly for a few minutes. Remove from heat and stir in lemon juice. Serve chilled.

COCONUT CHUTNEY
(Non dairy)

200 g (2 cups) unsweetened, untoasted, shredded coconut
500 mL (2 cups) yogurt
125 mL (1/2 cup) honey
5 mL (1 tsp.) sea salt
a sprinkle of coriander leaves
60 mL (4 tbs.) fresh ghee or light vegetable oil
5 mL (1 tsp.) mustard seeds
5 mL (1 tsp.) cumin seeds
a few curry leaves
5 mL (1 tsp.) asafoetida
5 mL (1 tsp.) cayenne or to taste
10 mL (2 tsp.) grated ginger root

1. Combine first 5 ingredients.
2. Prepare a chaunce in this way: Heat ghee or oil in a small cast iron frying pan until it just begins to smoke, add mustard seeds, when they begin to pop add other seeds. When they are lightly browned add curry leaves; when they are lightly toasted add asafoetida and cayenne, toast lightly then add ginger root, toasting it lightly. Stir everything into other ingredients. This is a must with dosa pancakes. (see index)

GREEN TOMATO CHUTNEY
(Non dairy)

4 green tomatoes washed and cut in 8 pieces
1 small green pepper washed, cut in half, white portion
   removed and cubed small
65 g (1/2 cup) washed raisins
60 mL (4 tbs.) fresh ghee or light vegetable oil
10 mL (2 tsp.) cumin seeds
5 mL (1 tsp.) turmeric
15 mL (1 tbs.) sea salt
60 mL (1/4 cup) lemon juice

1. Combine first 3 ingredients.
2. Prepare the chaunce in this way: Heat ghee or oil in sauce pan until it just begins to smoke, add cumin seeds, when browned add turmeric. Brown lightly then add first 3 ingredients.
3. Fry over medium heat stirring constantly until tomatoes are a bit softer, be careful not to overcook, they should be firm. Turn off heat and stir in salt and lemon juice. Serve chilled.

TOMATO CHUTNEY
(Non dairy)
10 medium tomatoes, washed and cubed
60 mL (4 tbs.) fresh ghee or light vegetable oil
5 mL (1 tsp.) mustard seeds
5 mL (1 tsp.) cumin seeds
5 mL (1 tsp.) fennel seeds
a few curry leaves
5 mL (1 tsp.) urad dal beans
5 mL (1 tsp.) ajawin seeds
10 mL (2 tsp.) instant tamarind
10 mL (2 tsp.) curry powder
5 mL (1 tsp.) asafoetida
10 mL (2 tsp.) cayenne or to taste
3 bay leaves
15 mL (1 tbs.) molasses
156 g (3/4 cup) demerara sugar
5 mL (1 tsp.) sea salt

1. Prepare a chaunce in this way: Heat ghee or oil in a sauce pan until it just begins to smoke, add mustard seeds, when they begin to pop add cumin and fennel seeds, brown lightly then add curry leaves. Again brown lightly then add urad dal beans and ajawin seeds, when everything is browned add tomatoes.
2. Mix instant tamarind with a little water to form a smooth paste and stir in with all remaining ingredients and cook over a medium heat stirring occasionally, uncovered until thick.
3. Serve chilled. If you like you may blend and store in fridge using as a ketchup.

APPLE CHUTNEY
(Non dairy)
3 large apples, washed, cored peeled and cubed
60 mL (4 tbs.) fresh ghee or light vegetable oil
5 mL (1 tsp.) mustard seeds
5 mL (1 tsp.) cumin seeds
5 mL (1 tsp.) fennel seeds
a few curry leaves
10 mL (2 tsp.) grated ginger root
5 mL (1 tsp.) asafoetida
5 mL (1 tsp.) cardamom powder
2.5 mL (1/2 tsp.) cinnamon
2.5 mL (1/2 tsp.) turmeric
10 mL (2 tsp.) cayenne or to taste
5 mL (1 tsp.) sea salt
156 mL (3/4 cup) demerara sugar

1. Prepare a chaunce in this way: Heat ghee or oil in a thick bottomed sauce pan until it just begins to smoke. Add mustard seeds, when they begin to pop add other seeds. Lightly brown and add curry leaves, then add ginger root and brown.
2. Add apples with powdered spices and cook over medium heat until mixture has thickened. Stir in salt and sweetener.

APPLE CHUTNEY #2
(Non dairy)

6 medium apples, washed, cored, peeled and cubed
125 mL (1/2 cup) water
raw sugar
5 mL (1 tsp.) citric acid
a pinch of salt

1. Add apples to thick bottomed pot, add water and cook covered until apples are soft.
2. Add contents of pot to blender and blend until smooth.
3. Add blended apples with an equal portion of sugar to pot, along with citric acid.
4. Cook over high heat uncovered, stirring constantly until mixture begins to thicken. Remove from heat, add salt and chill. Be careful, if you cook it after it begins to thicken it may be too hard when cooled.

MANGO CHUTNEY
(Non dairy)

3 large unripe mangoes, washed, peeled and grated
60 mL (4 tbs.) fresh ghee or light vegetable oil
10 mL (2 tsp.) mustard seeds
10 mL (2 tsp.) cumin seeds
250 mL (1 cup) water
5 mL (1 tsp.) sea salt

1. Prepare chaunce in this way: Heat ghee or oil in a thick bottomed sauce pan until it just begins to smoke. Add mustard seeds, when they begin to pop add cumin seeds, brown lightly then add mango. Fry a few minutes over medium heat stirring   constantly.
2. Add water and cook, stirring occasionally, until water is gone, then add sugar and salt and cook until it is thick. Serve chilled.

QUICK TAMARIND CHUTNEY
(UNCOOKED)
(Non dairy)

125 mL (1/2 cup) water
75 mL (5 tbs.) instant tamarind paste (available at
Indian food stores)
60 mL (4 tbs.) honey
3.6 mL (3/4 tsp.) sea salt
a sprinkle of pani pura masala (also available at Indian
food stores)

Add everything to blender, blend 30 seconds.

CORIANDER CHUTNEY
(UNCOOKED)
(Non dairy)

250 mL (1 cup) washed and chopped coriander leaves
5 mL (1 tsp.) cayenne or to taste
30 mL (2 tbs.) lemon juice
5 mL (1 tsp.) honey
2.5 mL (1/2 tsp.) turmeric
5 mL (1 tsp.) cumin seeds
60 mL (1/4 cup) salted peanuts
60 mL (1/4 cup) water

Blend everything until smooth.

GREEN PAPAYA CHUTNEY
(Non dairy)

1 large unripe papaya, washed, grated, unpeeled
250 mL (1 cup) water
210 gms (1 cup) raw sugar
5 mL (1 tsp.) cardamom powder
2.5 mL (1/2 tsp.) cayenne or to taste
2.5 mL (1/2 tsp.) sea salt

1. Add papaya to thick bottomed pot, add water, cook uncovered stirring occasionally until all the water is gone.
2. Add remaining ingredients and cook uncovered, stirring frequently until mixture is thick and looks a bit like marmalade. Serve chilled.

DATE CHUTNEY
(Non dairy)

380 g (2 cups) chopped soft dates (wash well)
250 mL (1 cup) water
30 mL (2 tbs.) lemon juice
30 mL (2 tbs.) honey
5 mL (1 tsp.) cayenne

Add everything to blender and blend until smooth. Use a rubber spatula to work dates to the blades.

PICKLES

Pickle Making Rules: Never touch pickles with hands while they are ripening, for germs from your hands can produce mold. Always sterilize jars with boiling water in a large pot. Turn off the heat and let the jars sit in the water for at least 10 minutes. Remove and dry fully with a clean cloth.

LEMON OR LIME PICKLE
(Non dairy)

7 seeded, unskinned lemons or limes cut in 8 pieces
125 mL (1/2 cup) ginger root cubed small
125 mL (1/2 cup) green chillies cut in very small pieces
60 mL (1/4 cup) sea salt
fresh lime juice
60 mL (1/4 cup) light vegetable oil

Mix all ingredients, add to sterilized jar, cover with lime juice and seal. Allow 2 weeks for ripening, shaking well every day.

CARROT PICKLE

4 scraped carrots cut in long stirps
15 mL (1 tsp.) sea salt
7.5 mL (1/2 tbs.) turmeric
15 mL (1 tbs.) ghee or light vegetable oil

Combine all ingredients in sterilized jar, seal and let sit a few hours in a warm spot.

RAITAS

A raita is a yogurt based dish that adds extra flavour to snacks, salads, or main dishes. It is usually not used as a dish by itself. Raitas are also very cooling and are popular in summer.

PAKORA RAITA

205 g (2 cups) chickpea flour
250 mL (1 cup) cold water
15 mL (1 tbs.) baking powder
ghee or light vegetable oil for deep frying
2.5 mL (1/2 tsp.) cayenne or to taste
5 mL (1 tsp.) sea salt
10 mL (2 tsp.) asafoetida
5 mL (1 tsp.) cumin powder
1 L (4 cups) yogurt

1. Combine the first 3 ingredients to form a thick batter.
2. Heat ghee or oil until it just begins to smoke.
3. Pour batter into colander and press through holes with back of spoon until top of ghee is covered with pieces ; fry in hot ghee or oil until they are lightly browned, remove and strain. Repeat until all the batter is fried.
4. Add pieces to bowl and add remaining ingredients, stir well.

BANANA RAITA

2 large bananas sliced
250 mL (1 cup) yogurt lightly beaten
15 mL (1 tbs.) lemon juice

Combine everything. Serve chilled.

POTATO OR CUCUMBER RAITA

3 medium potatoes (peeled) or
2 medium cucumbers, washed, peeled, and sliced
750 mL (3 cups) yogurt lightly beaten
15 mL (1 tbs.) lemon juice
a few coriander leaves
15 mL (1 tsp.) sea salt
2.5 mL (1/2 tsp.) cayenne
5 mL (1 tsp.) mustard seeds
5 mL (1 tsp.) cumin seeds
5 mL (1 tsp.) fennel seeds

1. If using potatoes, steam whole until soft. Grate and put in bowl, stir
   everything in but the seeds.
2. Prepare chaunce in this way: Heat a small cast iron frying pan over
   high heat. Add mustard seeds. When they begin to pop add other
   seeds. Cover with a wire screen and dry roast until lightly browned,
   then stir into other ingredients. Serve chilled.

10

I ndian
Sweets

BALARAMA BLISS

125 mL (1/2 cup) salted, melted butter
raw sugar to taste
260 g (2 cups) siftedwhole wheat flour
50 g (1/2 cup) lightly roasted coconut
a sprinkle of ground anise powder
sweetner to taste
500 mL (2 cups) sour cream
250 mL (1 cup) crushed pineapple, unsweetened and drained
190 g (1 cup) washed, chopped soft dates
138 g (1 cup) of your favourite nuts
5 mL (1 tsp.) vanilla

1. Heat oven to 177C (350F).
2. Combine butter, sugar, flour, coconut and anise and add cream to form a stiff dough.
3. Press in a thin rectangle shape onto a large well greased cookie sheet. Bake until browned.
4. Combine sweetner with sour cream, pineapple, dates, nuts and vanilla and spread evenly on crust. Bake in 191C (375F) oven for 10 minutes. Cut into about 2 dozen squares.

SWEET BALLS IN
ROSE WATER SYRUP
(Gulab-Jamun)

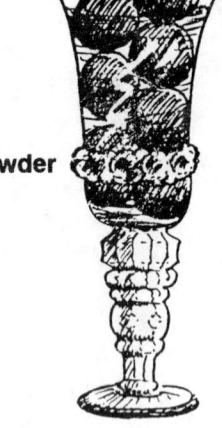

105 g (1 1/2 cups) non-instant, non-fat dry milk powder
38 g (5 tbs.) unbleached flour
7.5 mL (1/2 tbs.) baking powder
125 mL (1/2 cup) whole milk
fresh ghee or light vegetable oil for deep frying
1 L (4 cups) water
420 g (2 cups) raw sugar
rose water to taste

1. Mix together milk powder, flour and baking powder and add milk to form a sticky dough. Knead until smooth and just slightly sticky.
2. Break off dough in about 10 mL (3/4 tbs.) sizes and roll into very smooth balls. Work fast before the dough becomes dry.
3. Heat ghee or oil to 93C (200F) and add balls, when they drop in and go to the bottom and then rise, make sure they do not stick to bottom and burn. Cook for 1/2 hour turning often until the balls are dark brown.
4. Boil the sugar and water, reduce heat and add the balls. Cool at room temperature, adding some rose water to taste. If the balls collapse when added to sugar water it is because they are undercooked. Makes about 22.

CRUNCHY SWEET BALLS
(Lugloo)
(Non dairy)

200 g (2 cups) chickpea flour
15 mL (1 tbs.) baking powder
375 mL (1 1/2 cups) water (approx.)
fresh ghee or light vegetable oil for deep frying
210 g (1 cup) demerara sugar
190 g (1 cup) washed, chopped soft dates
430 mL (1 3/4 cup) water
150 g (1 cup) washed raisins
138 g (1 cup) chopped, roasted walnuts, almonds or cashews
a pinch of camphor to taste

1. Combine chickpea flour, baking powder and water to form a thin batter.
2. Punch holes in the bottom of an aluminium pie dish a bit larger than holes in a colander. Pour batter through holes and into the hot ghee or oil until the top of the ghee or oil is covered with pieces, which are called chicks. Fry until slightly browned, remove and strain. Repeat until all the batter is fried.
3. Combine sugar, water and dates in a thick bottomed pot and cook over medium heat until the mixture is thick and a bit sticky.
4. Stir in remaining ingredients. Roll into balls while still warm.

CRISP SWEET BREAD
(Takti)
(Non dairy)

240 g (2 cups) sifted unbleached flour
125 mL (1/2 cup) firm salted butter or margarine
10 mL (2 tsp) baking powder
60 mL (1/4 cup) water (approx.)
420 g (2 cups) demerara sugar
180 mL (3/4 cups) water
fresh ghee or light vegetable oil for deep frying

1. Cut the butter or margarine into the flour mixing it well with fingers. Add water to form a stiff dough and knead until very smooth.
2. Roll out evenly on a clean surface until approximately .63 cm (1/4 in.) thick and cut into bite-sized triangles.
3. Heat ghee or oil to medium temperature, add triangles and fry until browned on the outside and cooked through, but not hard. Remove and drain.
4. Cook the sugar and water until a little thick and slightly sticky. If you cook it too much, the sugar water will crystalize on the triangles.
5. Pour sugar syrup over triangles while still warm, making sure all pieces are well covered with the syrup. Makes about 20.

DIGESTIVE AID

60g (1/2 cup) ginger powder
30g (1/4 cup) gur
fresh ghee

Mix together gur and ginger powder until well blended. Add ghee or oil, so the mixture can be formed into small balls.

Gur is crystallized sugar cane juice (boiled to evaporate all the water). Gur is usually found at Indian stores.

FLUFFY SWEET CEREAL
(HALAVAH)
(Non dairy)

250 mL (1 cup) salted butter or soft margarine
360 g (2 cups) cream of wheat
1 L (4 cups) water
420 g (2 cups) raw sugar or demerara sugar
75 g (1/2 cup) golden raisins

1. Melt butter or margarine in a thick bottomed pot, and boil it a few minutes, being careful not to burn it. Turn the heat to low and slowly add the cream of wheat, stirring constantly. Cook this mixture on a low heat until it has the texture of wet sand. Stir frequently and be careful not to let it stick at the bottom and burn, thus spoiling the halavah.
2. When grains are ready, bring water to a boil. When water is boiling, turn heat to high on grains and add water, along with the raisins. Cook until it comes away from edges of pan, then add sugar. Cook a short while stirring often, turn heat to low, cover and steam 10 minutes. Serves 8.

VARIATIONS

1. Use 10 mL (2 tsp.) vanilla extract, stirring in after cooking.
2. Use strawberries instead of raisins, reducing water a little and using a bit more sugar.
3. Put small pieces of peeled apple in the water instead of raisins, or with the raisins, and 5 mL (1 tsp.) cinnamon. Mix a little water with the cinnamon to form a paste before adding it to the water so it mixes smoothly.
4. Grate orange or lemon peel and put in the boiling water.
5. Use milk instead of water, or be truly exotic and use half whipping cream , half milk; or use your favourite juice instead of water.
6. Add lots of curd to halavah after it is cooked.
7. Use your favourite nuts; a nice combination is walnuts with a little saffron.
8. Use any sweet spice that you desire, 5 mL (1 tsp.) of each, or 130 g (1 cup) carob powder added at the end of the cooking with a little extra sweetner.

9. Spread halavah in a pan and add a nice fruit topping such as cooked down mango pulp, lightly sweetened. (Available at Indian stores)
10. Use 1/2 chickpea flour, 1/2 cream of wheat.
11. Add grated carrots to the water.
12. Add 175 mL (3/4 cup) honey (instead of sugar), stir well, cover and let steam but don't cook.
13. Reduce sweetener by half and add a handful of chopped, soft dates to boiling water.

CHICKPEA HALAVAH
(Non dairy)

200 g (2 cups) sifted chickpea flour (sift before measuring)
250 mL (1 cup) salted butter or soft margarine
420 g (2 cups) raw sugar
500 mL (2 cups) water
150 g (1 cup) washed raisins

1. Melt butter or margarine in a large cast iron frying pan or wok. When it has bubbled for a few minutes add the chickpea flour. Stir well and turn down the heat to medium low. Cook slowly stirring often until the mixture becomes the color of peanut butter.
2. Combine the sugar, water and raisins in a pan and bring to a boil.
3. Pour the boiling liquid onto the cooking butter and chickpea flour combination and cook stirring constantly until it won't stick to the side of a pan. Serve warm. Serves 8.

SWEET BALLS IN YOGURT
(MALPOURI)

100 g (3/4 cup) chapati flour
90 g (3/4 cup) unbleached flour
210 g (1 cup) raw sugar
5 mL (1 tsp.) cinnamon
15 mL (1 tbs.) baking powder
water to make a thick batter
1 L (4 cups) thick yogurt
250 mL (1 cup) honey or any sweetner
fresh ghee or light vegetable oil for deep frying

1. Combine all dry ingredients and add enough water to make a thick batter. Fry as you would for chini wada (see next recipe), making sure it is cooked all the way through, and drain.
2. Mix together the yogurt and sweetner and just before serving stir in the fried pieces as they will not retain their crispness if left in the yogurt for very long. Serves 6.

VARIATIONS

Add your favourite fruit to the yogurt. Strawberries, bananas or raspberries go well with this recipe.

SWEET BALLS IN SYRUP
(CHINI WADA)
(Non dairy)

132 g (1 cup) urad dal flour
7.5 mL (1/2 tbs.) baking powder
250 mL (1 cup) water (approx.)
fresh ghee or light vegetable oil for deep frying
420 g (2 cups) demerara sugar
500 mL (2 cups) water

1. Combine urad dal flour and baking powder with just enough water to form a very thick batter.
2. Combine sugar and water and boil rapidly for 5 minutes.
3. Heat ghee or oil to medium heat. Be careful, if it is too hot, the balls will burn on the outside and not cook inside, and if not hot enough the balls will absorb too much ghee. Scoop out a full tablespoon of the mixture and slide off the spoon (using your finger) into the ghee. Continue this process until the top of the ghee is covered with the preparation. Brown them on one side turn over and brown the other side. If they come off the spoon a bit flat they will be able to stay turned after they are turned over; otherwise they may want to turn back to their original position. Scoop the wadas up and put directly into hot syrup. Serve at room temperature. Serves 5.

SWEET BALLS IN YOGURT
(DAHI WADA)

Following the previous recipe, after frying the wadas, simply add them to 1 L (4 cups) of yogurt with 375 mL (1 1/2 cups) of your favourite sweetener beaten in. Most importantly though, add the wadas to a
⁺ of hot water and let soak a few seconds. If you leave them too long
ˑill break up. Drain and carefully fold into the yogurt. If wadas
ˑaked in water before adding to the yogurt they will be very

SAFFRON PUDDING

500 mL (2 cups) whipping cream
125 mL (1/2 cup) milk
pinch of high quality saffron
105 g (1/2 cup) raw sugar

Combine all ingredients and boil until thick, stirring often in a good qualilty thick bottomed pot. Chill and serve straight or as a topping. This is a very rich and opulent sweet. Great for special occasions.

FRUIT IN SYRUP
(MOROBEE)
(Non dairy)

1 pineapple cubed
2 apples peeled and cubed
75 g (1/2 cup) dried fruit
375 mL (1 1/2 cups) water
demerara sugar to taste
4 crushed cardamom pods
a few saffron strands

Combine all ingredients in a thick bottomed pan and cook until the sugar water is thick. This can be used as a topping for Balarama Bliss.

RICH SWEET
(LADDU)
(Non dairy)

205 g (2 cups) chickpea flour
250 mL (1 cup) salted butter or soft margarine
250 mL (1 cup) honey (approx.) or   250 mL (1 cup) raw sugar
that has been powdered in a spice grinder.

1. Melt the butter or margarine, being careful not to burn it and gradually add the chickpea flour stirring until the mixture is smooth. Cook on low heat, stirring occasionally, until it turns to the color of peanut butter. The secret of good laddu is to be careful not to overcook it, as this destroys the flavor of the roasted chickpea flour.
2. Turn off heat and stir in honey or powdered raw sugar.
3. Pour into pan and cut into squares when cool or roll into balls. Makes about 2 dozen.

VARIATIONS

1. 160 g (1 cup) sesame seeds, put in at the beginning.
2. 100 g (1 cup) medium unsweetened roasted coconut added at the end, or unroasted and added near the beginning of the cooking.
3. 130 g (1 cup) raisins added at the end.
4. Laddu is also very palatable when made with unbleached white flour, just increase the butter by about 50 %.
5. You can also add roasted carob powder to laddu, about 65 g (1/2 cup).
6. Experiment with your favorite combinations and ingredients, also if you like you may add some sweet spices such as cardamom.
7. You may prepare a varaition called Dvaraka burfi by boiling together 375 mL (1 1/2 cups) brown sugar with 375 mL (1 1/2 cups) milk until thick. Then add to roasted chickpea flour and stir untill mixture starts to come away from the side of the pan. Pour into a pan and cut or roll into balls.

CELESTIAL BANANAS

7 large bananas, sliced lengthwise and halved
180 mL (3/4 cup) salted butter
One large pkg. of cream cheese
500 mL (2 cups) yogurt
demerara sugar to taste
cinnamon to taste

1. Heat oven to 191C (375F)
2. Fry all bananas in butter on both sides until slightly browned and drain well.
3. Put half the fried bananas down on a cookie sheet and dot with half the cream cheese, sprinkle with cinnamon and sugar. Repeat process. Top with yogurt and garnish with a little sweetener and cinnamon. Bake at 191C (375F) 20 minutes. Serve chilled. Serves 3.

CONDENSED MILK
TURNED INTO YOGURT
(MISTY DAHI)

2 L (8 cups) whole milk
250 mL (1 cup) yogurt
180 mL (3/4 cup) honey or raw sugar

1. Cook milk in a thick bottomed pot until about 500 mL (2 cups).
2. Cool the milk to 43C (110F), then beat in yogurt.
3. Cover and culture at same temperature for about 4 hours,
   (see pg. 8, step 3).
4. Stir in honey or raw sugar and chill.

BURFI

3 L (12 cups) whole milk
125 mL (1/2 cup) unsalted butter or fresh ghee
125 mL (1/2 cup) honey or raw sugar
5 mL (1 tsp.) vanilla extract (opt.)

1. Combine the milk and butter in a thick bottomed pot.
2. Cook on a high heat, stirring constantly until it boils, then stir occasionally until the milk begins to thicken. At this point you may add the raw sugar (don't add the honey as it is not good to cook honey. If using honey add at the end. Reduce the temperature to medium and stir constantly being very careful not to let it stick to the sides or bottom. Continue to stir until it is dry as possible.
3. Remove burfi from pot with a rubber spatula and spread as thinly as possible on a marble slab or table top. Let it cool and dry out for about one hour.
4. Knead the burfi until smooth with honey and vanilla, it should not be sticky. Roll burfi into balls or press into a pan and cut into squares. Makes about 2 dozen.

PERA

1. Add 105 g (1/2 cup) raw sugar at the beginning of cooking and 5 mL (1 tsp.) cardamom powder, add cardamom powder before heating the milk.
2. Follow directions for plain burfi omitting honey. Instead of rolling into balls, roll into 5 cm (2 in.) discs, dipping both sides in raw sugar.

RAISIN BURFI

Add 75 g (1/2 cup) raisins at the beginning of the cooking. Other kinds of dried fruit may also be used.

NUT BURFI

Add roasted chopped almonds, cashews, pistachios (or your favourite nuts) at the end of cooking.

DATE BURFI

1 L (4 cups) whole milk
285 g (1 1/2 cups) washed and chopped soft dates
30 mL (2 tbs.) unsalted butter or fresh ghee

Combine all ingredients in a thick bottomed pot and cook down stirring frequently until the preparation is as thick as possible. Towards the end reduce heat and stir constantly until the mixture doesn't stick to the bottom. Spread out thinly on a table to cool, then roll into balls.

CAROB DIP
(Non dairy)

138 g (1 cup) carob chips
45 mL (3 tbs.) warm water

Melt carob chips in top of double boiler, stir in water, and while still warm dip in and coat evenly your favorite sweets.

SANDESH

Prepare one batch of curd (see pg. 8) Instead of pressing curd squeeze water out of curd.

1. Knead until it is completely smooth, just like cream cheese. Add 1/3 as much sweetner and knead until smooth again.
2. Put Sandesh in a frying pan or thick bottomed pot and cook over a medium heat until it starts to separate from the sides and bottom of pot. Remove from pot and spread out thinly with spatula and let cool. Roll into balls or press into pan and cut into squares. Makes about 20 pieces.

VARIATIONS

1. Add 5 mL (1 tsp.) vanilla extract or cardamom powder before cooking.
2. Add some finely grated lemon, lime or orange rind before cooking.
3. Knead a little carob powder in before cooking.
4. Add carob chips or favorite roasted crushed nuts after cooking.
5. Prepare layered sandesh by preparing sandesh in 3 complimentary flavors and after cooking arrange in layers.
6. Roll out a thin layer of plain or flavored burfi and place a layer of flavored or plain sandesh on top, roll up and slice jelly roll style.

SWEET CURD BALLS IN SYRUP
(RASAGULLAS)

Prepare 1 batch of curd (see pg. 8)
2 L (8 cups) water
840 g (4 cups) raw sugar

1. Prepare curd as above and knead until smooth. Roll into 20 smooth balls.
2. Combine water and sugar and bring to boil. Add the curd balls, cover and boil on a high heat until the rasagullas have stopped expanding - about 10 minutes. Serve chilled.

NOTE: Rasagullas are difficult to prepare due to the problem of knowing when they are cooked. When done properly they will make a squeaky sound when bitten into and at the same time they will be soft. Practice makes perfect.

VARIATIONS

1. Make Rasamali by adding Rasagullas to thick cream or whipping cream.
2. Make Ksircon Balls by covering Rasagullas in a layer of fresh pliable burfi.
3. Put a piece of rock candy inside each Rasagulla.

SWEET RICE

1.5 L (6 cups) whole milk
24 g (1/4 cup) well washed basmati or other white rice
   (soaked 24 hours)
125 mL (1/2 cup) honey or raw sugar

1. Bring milk and soaked rice to boil in thick bottomed pot, stirring frequently while heating.
2. Boil over medium heat stirring occasionally, especially the bottom to avoid milk from sticking. Once the milk starts to boil it needs less stirring than when heating up, as the boiling action tends to stir it somewhat.
3. Cook until the rice is very soft and milk is creamy. You may have to add water during cooking, as milk may thicken before rice is cooked. In approximately 1 hour the preparation will be done; then stir in the sweetner. Serve as cold as possible - the colder the sweet rice the better the taste. You should be able to pour the final product.

VARIATIONS

1. Mix 5 mL (1 tsp.) cardamom powder with milk before heating, or add 5 mL (1 tsp.) vanilla extract at the end.
2. Add your favorite fruit after sweet rice has cooled, such as 125 mL (1/2 cup) frozen strawberries in syrup, with or without the flavoring in variation #1.
3. Add 25 g (1/4 cup) untoasted unsweetened coconut with rice.
Tapioca: Prepare like sweet rice, but be carefull; tapioca sticks more than sweet rice and cooks faster. The best tapioca is very small and is found in Indian stores, but you can also purchase seed tapioca at large supermarkets.

CONDENSED MILK
(KHEER)

2 L (8 cups) whole milk
105 g (1/2 cup) raw sugar

Boil milk and sugar together in a thick pot, stirring constantly until it boils, and thereafter occasionally until the milk develops a thick consistency. (At first the milk may tend to boil over the top of the pot - in that case dip a ladle in and out of milk to prevent it from spilling over). Stir occasionally after removing from heat to prevent a skin from forming.

Refrigerate until cold, or freeze for quick ice cream. Kheer may be as thick, or as thin as you like, but in India it is served so thick it can be eaten with a spoon.

VARIATIONS

1. Add a few strands of saffron at beginning, and a chopped banana after cooled.
2. Firni: 30 mL (2 tbs.) rice flour is whisked in after cooking.
3. Crumple in a handful of well pressed curd after kheer is cooked and stir well, for preparation of curd see pg. 8.
4. Fruit of your choice may be added, but please avoid melons.

CONDENSED YOGURT
(SHIRKHAND)

2 L (8 cups) thick yogurt
raw sugar
saffron or nutmeg flavoring
small pieces of dried fruit or
small pieces of banana or
small pieces of favourite roasted nuts or
finely grated lemon rind

1. Place the yogurt on thin cotton or thin muslin, firmly tie together the four corners and suspend above a bowl. Let it drip for at least 6 hours (longer for thicker shirkhand up to 12 hours.)
2. Scrape shirkhand from the cloth and add 1/3 as much sweetener, or to taste. Add your favourite flavor, fruit and nuts.

MAHA SWEET

105 g (1/2 cup) demerara sugar
10 mL (2 tsp.) salted butter
250 mL (1 cup) whole milk
100 g (1 cup) roasted, shredded coconut
125 mL (1/2 cup) whole milk approx.
60 g (1/2 cup) unbleached flour
7.5 mL (1/2 tbs.) cardamom powder
105 g (1/2 cup) demerara sugar
350 mL (1 cup) water
fresh ghee or light vegetable oil

1. Combine sugar, butter, 1 cup milk and coconut and cook down In a thick bottomed pot until it becomes dry and doesn't stick to the bottom of the pot. Spread in a pan and chill. Roll into balls.
2. Heat ghee or oil until it almost smokes.
3. Combine flour and cardamom and add milk to form a thin batter. Dip
4. balls in batter and fry until they are a golden brown color.
5. While the balls are frying, boil sugar and water rapidly for about 5 minutes.
6. Take balls out of ghee and pour syrup over top. These are also very good served in kheer, mentioned on previous page. Serves four.

SIMPLY WONDERFUL SWEET

260 g (2 cups) non-instant, non-fat dry milk powder.
250 mL (1 cup) unsalted butter or fresh ghee
250 mL (1 cup) honey or 220g (2 cups) raw sugar that has
    been powdered in a spice grinder
75 g (1/2 cup) approx. chopped nuts, raisins or carob powder

1. Melt butter or ghee and stir in honey or sugar until a smooth consistency is obtained. Add milk powder gradually and mix well, adding nuts or raisins. If using carob, mix well with milk powder.
2. Squeeze into 2.5 cm (1 in.) balls. Makes about 2 dozen.

VARIATION

You may form simply wonderfuls in the shape of cookies and bake at 149C (300F) for 10-12 minutes on a lightly buttered cookie sheet.

11

Cakes & pies

CAKE COMMENT

When baking your cake, all liquids should be cold, and stirring should be in one direction, about 300 strokes.

BASIC WHITE CAKE

240 g (2 cups) unbleached flour
15 mL (1 tbs.) baking powder
2.5 mL (1/2 tsp.) sea salt
125 mL (1/2 cup) soft butter, unsalted
210 g (1 cup) demerara sugar
5 mL (1 tsp.) vanilla
60 mL (4 tbs.) yogurt or sour cream
175 mL (3/4 cup) milk

1. Grease well the bottom of a 20 cm (8 in.) square pan and flour, removing the excess. Heat oven to 177C (350F).
2. Beat together butter, sugar, yogurt and vanilla in a good sized mixing bowl until fluffy.
3. Combine all dry ingredients, sifting them together.
4. Add 1/4 of flour mixture to butter mixture and mix until smooth; add 1/3 of the milk and mix until smooth. Continue until all ingredients are used.
5. Spread in a prepared pan and bake for 40-45 minutes on rack just below centre, no peeking for 30 minutes. To test the doneness, press top of cake with a finger tip. If the mark or imprint made by the finger springs back or does not remain, the cake is done. You can double check the consistency by sticking a cake tester or a wooden pick in the centre of the cake. If it comes out clean and dry, the cake is done.
6. When the cake is done remove at once and set on a wire rack. Let stand 10 minutes, then loosen the cake around the edges with a metal spatula. Place another cooling rack on top of the cake and turn both racks (the cake between them) upside down. The top of the cake will be right side up. Let cake cool fully and frost with your favorite frosting.

    For variety add 15 mL (1 tbs.) toasted poppy seeds to batter, grated orange rind, or mix 65 g (1/2 cup) carob powder with flour.

SPICE CAKE

240 g (2 cups) unbleached flour
15 mL (1 tbs.) baking powder
2.5 mL (1/2 tsp.) sea salt
2.5 mL (1/2 tsp.) cinnamon
2.5 mL (1/2 tsp.) allspice
2.5 mL (1/2 tsp.) nutmeg
1.2 mL (1/4 tsp.) cloves
125 mL (1/2 cup) unsalted butter, softened

210 g (1 cup) demerara sugar
2.5 mL (1/2 tsp.) vanilla
60 mL (4 tbs.) yogurt or sour cream
180 mL (3/4 cup) milk

1. Grease well the bottom of a 20 cm (8 in.) square pan and flour, removing the excess. Heat oven to 177C (350F).
2. Beat together until fluffy butter, sugar, vanilla and yogurt.
3. Sift together all dry ingredients.
4. Add 1/4 of flour mixture to butter mixture and mix until smooth; add

1/3 of the milk and mix until smooth. Continue until all flour is mixed and a thick batter is achieved.

5. Follow steps 5 and 6 for basic cake, frost as desired.

SOUR CREAM CAKE

180 g (1 1/2 cups) unbleached flour
15 mL (1 tbs.) baking powder
250 mL (1 cup) sour cream
5 mL (1 tsp.) baking soda
263 g (1 1/4 cups) demerara sugar
125 mL (1/2 cup) unsalted butter, softened
5 mL (1 tsp.) vanilla
125 mL (1/2 cup) cold water
53 g (1/4 cup) demerara sugar
5 mL (1 tsp.) cinnamon
35 g (1/4 cup) chopped nuts

1. Grease well the bottom of a 20 cm (8 in.) pan and flour, removing the excess. Heat oven to 177C (350F).
2. Sift together flour and baking powder, mix sour cream and baking soda, let rise.
3. Beat together sugar and butter until fluffy, then beat in the vanilla.
4. Follow exactly step 4 for basic white cake using water instead of milk.
5. Fold in sour cream.
6. Pour 1/2 of batter in pan, sprinkle on remaining ingredients, swirl, add other 1/2.
7. Follow steps 5 and 6 for basic cake.
   Bake 45-50 minutes.

BANANA CAKE
(Non dairy)

180 g (1 1/2 cup) unbleached flour
15 mL (1 tbs.) baking powder
2.5 mL (1/2 tsp.) baking soda
2.5 mL (1/2 tsp.) sea salt (less if using margarine)
.6 mL (1/8 tsp.) cloves
5 mL (1 tsp.) cinnamon
2.5 mL (1/2 tsp.) nutmeg
125 mL (1/2 cup) unsalted butter or soft margarine
160 g (3/4 cup) demerara sugar
30 mL (2 tbs.) yogurt or sour cream (optional)
250 mL (1 cup) mashed banana
5 mL (1 tsp.) vanilla
30 mL (2 tbs.) water (approx.)
honey for topping

1. Grease the bottom of a 20 cm.(8 in.) square pan and flour, removing the excess. Heat oven to 177C (350F).
2. Sift together all dry ingredients.
3. Beat together butter,or margarine, sugar and next 4 ingredients until smooth.
4. Divide liquids in half. Add 1/4 of flour mixture to one half of liquids and beat until smooth; add 1/3 of other half of liquids and mix until smooth, continue until all ingredients are used. The batter should be on the thick side. If too thick add a bit of water.
5. Follow exactly steps 5 and 6 in the basic cake on page 78, but do not frost, instead top with honey. Be careful, if you cut this cake before it is cold it may fall.

VARIATIONS

Peaches, apricots or apple sauce may be used instead of bananas.

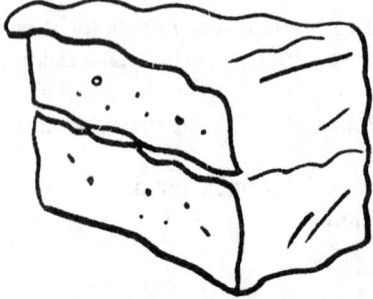

CARROT CAKE

180 g (1 1/2 cups) unbleached flour
15 mL (1 tbs.) baking powder
2.5 mL (1/2 tsp.) sea salt
5 mL (1 tsp.) cinnamon
1.2 mL (1/4 tsp.) nutmeg
pinch of allspice
125 mL (1/2 cup) unsalted butter, softened
210 g (1 cup) demerara sugar
60 mL (4 tbs.) yogurt or sour cream
5 mL (1 tsp.) vanilla
1 or 2 orange peels grated
1 grated carrot
75 g (1/3 cup) milk

1. Grease well the bottom of a 20 cm.(8 in.) square pan and flour, removing the excess. Heat oven to 177C (350F).
2. Sift together first 6 ingredients.
3. Beat together butter and sugar until fluffy, beat in yogurt and vanilla, fold in grated orange peel and grated carrots.
4. Add 1/4 of flour mixture and mix until smooth; add 1/3 of milk until smooth. Continue until all ingredients are used.
5. Follow steps 5 and 6 for basic white cake on page 78.

CHEESE CAKE

2 large size pkgs. cream cheese
1 can of Eagle Brand condensed milk
sea salt to taste (opt.)
5 mL (1 tsp.) vanilla
60 mL (1/4 cup) lemon juice
290 g (2 cups) Corn Flakes or granola blended
salted melted butter
honey to taste
cinnamon to taste
2.5 mL (1/2 tsp.) vanilla
5 mL (1 tsp.) raw sugar
250 mL (1 cup) sour cream
fruit and or whipped cream

1. Soften cream cheese and beat until creamy. Then beat in Eagle Brand along with the salt, lemon juice and vanilla until well mixed.
2. Prepare a crust made from either blended granola or Corn Flake crumbs with butter added to bind together, along with honey to taste. Press into a 23 cm.(9 in.) shell.
3. Pour cream cheese mixture on top and dust with cinnamon.
4. Combine vanilla, sugar and sour cream and pour on top of cream cheese mixture.
5. Bake for about 10 minutes in medium oven until firm, cool down and top with fruit and or whipped cream.

UPSIDE DOWN CAKE

240 g (2 cups) unbleached flour
15 mL (1 tbs.) baking powder
2.5 mL (1/2 tsp.) sea salt
125 g (1/2 cup) unsalted butter, softened
210 g (1 cup) demerara sugar
60 mL (4 tbs.) yogurt or sour cream
5 mL (1 tsp.) vanilla
175 mL (3/4 cup) milk

TOPPING

Combine
75 mL (1/3 cup) melted unsalted butter
1/2 pineapple cut in thin chunks or
2 medium apples peeled and sliced

1. Add topping mix to a 23 cm. (9 in.) pan. If using apples, sprinkle on 2.5 mL (1/2 tsp.) cinnamon.
2. Heat oven to 177C (350F).
3. Beat together until fluffy sugar, butter, yogurt and vanilla.
4. Sift together dry ingredients.
5. Add 1/4 of flour mixture to butter mixture and mix until smooth; add 1/3 of the milk and mix until smooth. Continue until all flour is mixed in and batter is thick.
6. Follow steps 5 and 6 for basic cake on pg. 78.

NOTE:

Upside down cakes usually take about 50% longer to bake.

VARIATION

Instead of apples or pineapple, use your favourite fruit, spicing and sweetening to taste, or use your favourite nuts with/or instead of fruit.

FROSTINGS

Frostings are very important to give that final touch, and add a bit of glamour to the cake. There are no hard and fast rules in frosting cakes, just let your imagination go. To be creative use fruit spreads, jam, instant puddings and fillings, pie fillings, date fillings, honey, etc.

HOW TO MAKE
A SHORT-CUT CAKE BATTER

125 mL (1/2 cup) melted unsalted butter
105 g (1/2 cup) demerara sugar
125 mL (1/2 cup) whole milk
5 mL (1 tsp.) vanilla
240 g (2 cups) unbleached flour
15 mL (1 tbs.) baking powder
5 mL (1 tsp.) sea salt

1. Mix together first 4 ingredients.
2. Mix together last 3 ingredients.
3. Beat dry ingredients into wet and pour into cake pan as directed in the basic cake recipe on pg. 78.

RAM GOVINDA'S MEXICAN CAKE

120 g (1 cup) unbleached flour
150 g (1 cup) corn meal
20 mL (4 tsp.) baking powder
2.5 mL (1/2 tsp.) sea salt
2.5 mL (1/2 tsp.) cayenne (or to taste)
32 g (1/4 cup) skim milk powder
60 mL (1/4 cup) raw sugar
125 mL (1/2 cup) unsalted butter
250 mL (1 cup) milk
1 medium green pepper, washed, cut in half, white
   portion removed, and minced.

1. Grease well the bottom of a 20 cm. (8 in.) square pan and flour, removing the excess. Heat oven to 177C (350F).
2. Mix together first 6 ingredients. Mix together remaining ingredients.
3. Mix both together, just enough to moisten. Don't beat.
4. Follow steps 5 and 6 for basic white cake on pg. 78.

TIPS ON PIE MAKING

When making pastry doughs, always measure very carefully, follow the recipe exactly. Sprinkle water slowly; if you add too much, more flour will be needed. As you sprinkle water over shortening-flour mixture, lift mixture with a fork from the bottom of the bowl. Sprinkle water and as pieces stick together set them aside, continue sprinkling until other dry pieces stick together. Press together all the dampened pieces to form a ball that will clean the bowl; if this does not happen, too much water has been added. Dampen table top, put down a sheet of waxed paper then the dough. Roll dough 12 cm. (5 in.) in diameter. Cover with more waxed paper and roll out to .33 cm. (1/8 in.) rolling from centre out. Peel off top paper, invert pan over dough, turn right side up, peel off paper, and fit in pan. If you roll in flour, it will tend to make the crust tough. The top crust is rolled out like the bottom crust.

STANDARD PIE CRUST
(Non dairy)

240 g (2 cups) unbleached flour
3.7 mL (3.4 tsp.) sea salt
250 mL (1 cup) hard vegetable shortening
    or hard unsalted butter
45-60 mL (3-4 tbs.) ice water

1. Sift the flour and salt into a bowl. Cut shortening 0r butter into small chunks and drop over mixture; cut shortening into flour with a pastry blender or 2 knives. The mixture should have the texture of fairly course cornmeal. Gradually sprinkle with water and stir with a fork until evenly moistened. Press together until mixture cleans bowl and forms a ball. Cut off 1/2 of dough for top crust. Roll out as instructed in paragraph above. Trim edge evenly with pan.

2. Fill crust with filling. Rol! top crust as for bottom crust. Dampen edges of lower crust, set top in place letting it extend 1.2 cm. (1/2 in.) beyond rim. Fold extended edge under moistened edge, and press. Crimp edge and poke holes in an artistic way on the top to let the steam escape.

3. Bake 218C (425F) for 20 minutes, then reduce heat to 177C (350F) and continue baking 10 to 20 minutes, depending on filling until browned lightly. For unfilled shells, prick and bake at 218C (425F) 15 to 20 minutes. Put loosely in pan.

HOW TO MAKE
A QUICK SWEET CRUST
(Non dairy)

Mix together 180 g (1 1/2 cups) unbleached flour with a pinch of baking powder and about 105 g (1/2 cup) raw sugar. Melt some salted butter or oil and add to achieve a consistency that can be pressed into a buttered pan to form a crust. Bake in a moderate oven until browned and top with your favourites to make a nice sweet pie.

SHORTBREAD

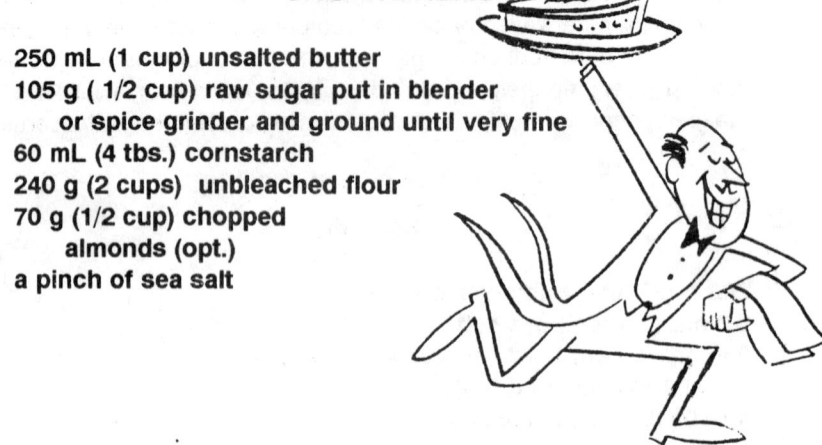

250 mL (1 cup) unsalted butter
105 g (1/2 cup) raw sugar put in blender
   or spice grinder and ground until very fine
60 mL (4 tbs.) cornstarch
240 g (2 cups) unbleached flour
70 g (1/2 cup) chopped
     almonds (opt.)
a pinch of sea salt

1. Preheat oven to 149C (300F).
2. Cream together, butter and sugar, work in other ingredients. Knead until smooth.
3. Mold into 10 to 12 cakes 1.2 cm. (1/2 in.) thick, prick top with fork.
4. Bake in preheated oven 45 to 50 minutes or until light brown.

APPLE PIE
(Non dairy)

4 to 5 medium apples, cored, peeled and sliced
210 g (1 cup) demerara sugar, firmly packed or to taste
15 mL (1 tbs.) unbleached flour
5 mL (1 tsp.) cinnamon or to taste
a pinch of nutmeg
2.5 mL (1/2 tsp.) sea salt, or to taste
30 mL (2 tbs.) unsalted butter or soft magarine
a few raisins to taste

1. Prepare crust as described on pages 85-86.
2. Mix together very well sugar, flour, cinnamon, nutmeg and salt.
3. Mix in apples.
4. Preheat oven to 218C (425F).
5. Place fruit mixture evenly in a pastry lined pie pan. Dot with butteror margarine.
6. Adjust top crust (see step 2 on previous page) and seal well. You can prevent the edge of the pie browning too much by covering with a thin strip of aluminium foil. Bake in the centre of the oven as described on previous page.

RHUBARB PIE

3 or 4 rhubarbs washed and chopped small
210 g (1 cup) raw sugar or to taste
30 mL (2 tbs.) yogurt
30 mL (2 tbs.) unbleached flour

1. Prepare crust as described on pages 85-86.
2. Preheat oven to 232C (450F).
3. Combine sugar, flour and yogurt and add to rhubarb.
4. Add rhubarb to pastry shell.
5. Adjust the top crust.
6. Bake on bottom rack 10 minutes, then bake 45-50 minutes at 177C (350F), on middle rack.

BERRY PIES

(Non dariy)

**750 mL (3 cups) strawberries, raspberries, blueberries,
blackberries or loganberries
105 g (1/2 cup) raw sugar or to taste
30 g (4 tbs.) unbleached flour
a pinch of salt
15 mL (1 tbs.) unsalted butter or soft margarine**

1. Prepare crust as described on pages 85 & 86.
2. Preheat oven to 205 C (400F)
3. Pile berries in pastry shell.
4. Mix together sugar, flour and salt, sprinkle over berries. Dot with butter or margarine.
5. Adjust top crust.
6. Bake on bottom rack until golden brown, about 35 minutes.

TARTS

Prepare pastry as described on page 85 and 86, but cut dough 2.5 cm (1 in.) larger than tart well. Ease in gently, but do not stretch. Add filling and bake.

DEVA APPLES

**4 tart apples, medium size, peeled and sliced
105 g (1/2 cup) demerera sugar, or to taste
2.5 mL (1/2 tsp.) cinnamon
30 mL (2 tbs.) butter, unsalted
standard baking powder
biscuit dough (see index)
cream
sea salt**

1. Heat oven to 177 C (350 F.)
2. Arrange apples in baking dish, sprinkle on cinnamon, salt and sugar. Dot with butter.
3. Roll out biscuit dough (see index) on waxed paper, the size of pan and put on top of apples. Prick with fork.
4. Bake in preheated oven 45 minutes or until browned lightly.
5. Serve upside down, top with cream.

PIE FILLINGS
CREAM FILLING

62 g (1/2 cup) cornstarch
210 g (1 cup) raw sugar
500 mL (2 cups) milk
15 mL (1tbs.) unsalted butter
5 mL (1 tsp.) vanilla
bananas
whipped cream (opt.)

1. Combine cornstarch with a little water to make a paste, stir sugar into cold milk, beat in cornstarch. Heat milk in a thick bottomed pot over medium heat, stirring constantly, until milk is thick.
2. Remove from heat stir in vanilla and butter, cool.
3. When cool stir in sliced bananas, pour into pre-baked pie shell or tart shell (see pages 85 and 86) with whipped cream if desired.

SOUR CREAM FILLING

30 mL (2 tbs.) cornstarch
250 g (1 cup) cold milk
60 mL (4tbs.) sour cream
15 mL 1 tbs.) unsalted butter
5 mL (1tsp.) vanilla

1. Combine first 2 ingredients in a thick bottemed sauce pan. Gradually add to cold milk in a saucepan.
2. Stir constantly over medium heat until mixture is thickened. Let bubble for one minute.
3. Beat in sour cream and cook for about 2 minutes, stirring constantly.
4. Remove from heat. Blend in butter and vanilla.

RAISIN PIE FILLING
(Non dariy)

Blend 300 g (2 cups) firmly packed raisins with 250 mL (1 cup) water. Add 105 g (1/2 cup) raw sugar (approx.) and cook until it thickens. Add salted butter to taste or soft margarine to taste.

12

Cookies & Candies

BAR COOKIES

Bar cookies are baked like cakes, then cut in a bar shape or square. Be careful to use the correct pan size. If the pan is too big, the dough will be too thin and overcook. If it's too small, the dough will be too thick and not cook inside. Don't overmix brownies as this gives a hard, crusty top. Spread the dough evenly in the pan. Be careful not to overcook. Check the consistency of brownies by gently pressing the top of the cookie with your finger tip. (If your finger makes a slight dent or imprint that remains, the cookies are done). Do this a few minutes before they are expected to be done. Cool bar cookies at least 10 minutes before cutting them. If they are cut too soon they may crumble.

FUDGE BROWNIES

60 g (1/2 cup) roasted carob powder
plus 60 mL (4 tbs.) liquid
75 mL (1/3 cup) salted butter (softened)
88 g (3/4 cup), unbleached flour
15 mL (1 tbs.) baking powder
210 g (1 cup) raw sugar
60 mL (4 tbs.) yogurt
5 mL (1 tsp.) vanilla
60 g (1/2 cup) chopped nuts

1. Grease lightly a 20 cm (8 in.) square pan with unsalted butter or oil.
2. Heat oven to 177C (350F)
3. Combine carob and liquid with butter. Heat over low temperature until butter is melted, cool to lukewarm and add vanilla.
4. Sift together flour and baking powder.
5. Beat together sugar and yogurt until light.
6. Beat carob-butter mixture into yogurt-sugar mixture. Stir in the flour mixture and nuts. Mix well.
7. Spread evenly on the pan and bake on centre rack of preheated oven for 20 to 25 minutes. When done the crust on top will have a dull look.
8. Remove from oven and cool fully before cutting.

VARIATIONS

1. Bake in a 23 cm (9 in.) round layer pan. Cool and cut pie style.
2. Top with ice cream, maple syrup or fruit sauce.

DATE SQUARES
(Non dairy)

250 mL (1 cup) salted butter (softened) or soft margarine
220 g (1 cup) firmly packed demerara sugar (or to taste)
175 g (1 1/2 cups), unbleached flour
2.5 mL (1/2 tsp.) baking soda
150 g (1 1/2 cups) quick oats
30 mL (2 tbs.) yogurt (opptional)
380 g (2 cups) chopped, washed soft dates
250 mL (1 cup) water
52 g (1/4 cup) demerara sugar
10 mL (2 tsp.) lemon juice

1. Grease well a 20 cm(8 in.) cake pan with unsalted butter or oil. Heat oven to 177C (350F).
2. Combine last 4 ingredients in a small saucepan, cover and simmer until dates are soft.
3. Beat together butter or margarine and sugar.
4. Sift together flour and baking soda and add to butter or margarine and sugar.
5. Add rolled oats and yogurt (if desired) and mix everything with your hands.
6. Place half the mixture in pan and spread smoothly, patting down firmly.
7. Spread on filling, cover smoothly, patting down firmly.
8. Cover smoothly with the rest of crumb mixture and pat lightly.
9. Bake in a preheated oven about 35 minutes or until lightly browned. Cool then cut. Any berries or other fruit, such as apples, may be used instead of dates.

PINEAPPLE SQUARES

125 mL (1/2 cup) salted butter, softened
52 g (1/4 cup) demerara sugar
180 g (1 1/2 cups) unbleached flour
60 mL (4 tbs.) cold milk (approx.)
250 mL (1 cup) crushed pineapple
kheer recipe - very thick (see index)
100 g (1 cup) shredded coconut, lightly toasted

1. Grease well a 20 cm (8 in.) square pan. Heat oven to 177C (350F).
2. Beat together butter and sugar until fluffy, mix in flour with hands until well mixed, add milk to form a soft dough.
3. Press dough into pan, prick all over with a fork. Bake 25 minutes, or until browned, in a preheated oven.
4. Remove from oven, combine last three ingredients and spread evenly on top.
5. Bake 25 minutes, cool 10 minutes and cut.

APPLE CRISP
(Non dairy)

5 or 6 medium apples, peeled, cored and sliced.
60 mL (1/4 cup) water
5 mL (1 tsp.) cinnamon
a pinch of sea salt
75 mL (1/3 cup) melted unsalted butter or soft margarine
105-210 g (1/2 - 1 cup) demerara sugar
   (according to sweetness of apples)
150 g (1 1/2 cup) quick oats

1. Heat oven to 177C (350F)
2. Spread apples evenly on pan and sprinkle water over top with cinnamon.
3. Mix together last 4 ingredients until a crumb like consistency is attained. Cover the top.
4. Bake in preheated oven for 45 minutes or until apples are soft. This is nice served warm, with cream. Other fruit can be substituted.

DROP COOKIES

To make this type of cookie soft dough is pushed and dropped from a spoon onto a baking sheet. Before baking a whole batch of cookies, bake a few. If they spread out too much, add a little flour to the dough. If cookies spread too much the edges will be too thin and burn. If cookies don't spread enough, they will be dry and less tender.

Drop cookies are easy to dress up; just press nuts or candied cherries on the centre of each cookie before baking. You may cover the baked and cooled cookies with cake frosting.

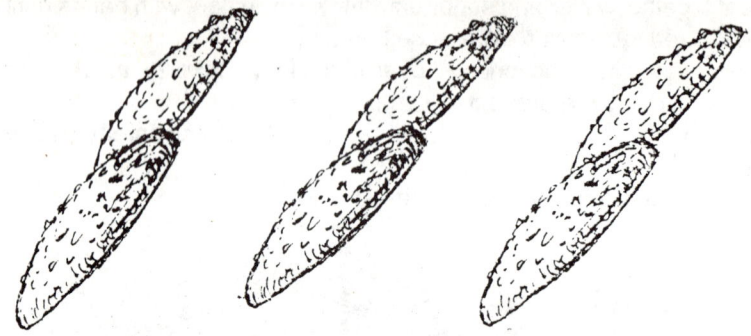

CAROB CHIP COOKIES

120 g (1 cup) unbleached flour
1.2 mL (1/4 tsp.) sea salt
2.5 mL (1/2 tsp.) baking soda
125 mL (1/2 cup) unsalted softened butter
210 g (1 cup) demerara sugar
30 mL (2 tbs.) yogurt
2.5 mL (1/2 tsp.) vanilla
110 g (1/2 cup) carob chips
60 g (1/2 cup) chopped walnuts

1. Lightly grease cookie sheet. Heat oven to 177C (350F).
2. Sift together flour, salt and baking soda.
3. Mix 30 mL (2 tbs.) dry ingredients with chips and nuts.
4. Add dry ingredients to liquids, butter and sugar, mix well, fold in chips and nuts.
5. Drop by 15 mL (1 tbs.) 5 cm (2 in.) apart on greased cookie sheets.
6. Bake in preheated oven 8-10 minutes, or until a slight dent remains when you lightly touch the cookie. Makes about fifteen cookies.

SIMPLE DROP COOKIES

150 mL (2/3 cup) unsalted butter, softened
156 g (3/4 cup) raw sugar
60 mL (4 tbs.) yogurt
120 g (1 cup) unbleached flour
60 g (1/2 cup) corn starch
15 mL (1tbs.) baking powder
1.2 mL (1/4 tsp.) sea salt or to taste
100 g (1 cup) roasted coconut

1. Lightly grease cookie sheet. Heat oven to 177C (350F)
2. Beat together butter and sugar until fluffy, with yogurt and vanilla.
3. Sift together flour, corn starch, baking powder. Stir in coconut.
4. Stir flour mixture into butter mixture, mix well.
5. Drop mixture by small 15 mL (1 tbs.) 5 cm (2 in.) apart on cookie sheet.
6. Bake in preheated oven 10-12 minutes or until browned on the bottom. This makes about 20 cookies.

MOLDED COOKIES

In preparing molded cookies you shape the stiff dough with your hands, often into balls. To keep it from sticking to your hands the dough is often chilled in the refrigerator. Sometimes the dough is flattened on a baking sheet, using a fork or a glass bottom, dipped in sugar. A thumb print may be put in the cookie, then nuts or fruit are inserted.

CAROB COOKIES

250 mL (1 cup) unsalted butter, softened
210 g (1 cup) demerara sugar
90 mL (6tbs.) yogurt
1.2 mL (1/4 tsp.) sea salt
7.5 mL (1/2 tbs.) baking soda
270 g (2 1/4 cups) unbleached flour
40 g (1/3 cup) sifted roasted carob
2.5 mL (1/2 tsp.) vanilla

1. Grease cookie sheets. Heat oven to 177C (350F).
2. Beat butter and sugar together with yogurt and vanilla until very fluffy.
3. Sift together salt, flour and carob.
4. Stir flour into liquids, mixing well.
5. Press onto cookie sheet 2.5cm (1 in.) apart. Bake in a preheated oven for 10-12 minutes or until browned on bottom. Makes 2 dozen cookies.

VARIATION
(Non dairy)

Omit carob and add same amount of raisins.

GINGER COOKIES
(Non dairy)

175 mL (3/4 cup) softened, unsalted butter or soft margarine
210 g (1 cup) demerara sugar
60 mL (1/4 cup) molasses
240 g (2 cups) unbleached flour
1.2 mL (1/4 tsp.) sea salt
7.5 mL (1/2 tbs.) baking soda
2.5 mL (1/4 tsp.) nutmeg
1.2 mL (1/4 tsp.) cloves
5 mL (1 tsp.) cinnamon
10 mL (2 tsp.) ginger powder
45-60 mL (3 or 4 tbs.) milk or water

1. Preheat oven to 177C (350F). Lightly grease cookie sheet with shortening.
2. Cream together sugar and butter or margarine with molasses.
3. Mix together all remaining ingredients except milk.
4. Stir dry mixture into butter mixture, mix well, and add milk to form a stiff dough.
5. Form into 15 discs and dip tops in sugar. Arrange on cookie sheet 2.5 cm (1 in.) apart.
6. Bake in preheated oven for 10 minutes or until slightly browned on bottom.

VARIATIONS

1. Cut out to form ginger bread men.
2. For ginger snaps make a little thinner.

PEANUT BUTTER COOKIES
(Non dairy)

125 mL (1/2 cup) softened unsalted butter
210 g (1 cup) demerara sugar
30 mL (2 tbs.) yogurt (opp)
150 mL (2/3 cup) peanut butter
2.5 mL (1/2 tsp.) vanilla
2.5 mL (1/2 tsp.) salt
2.5 mL (1/2 tsp.) baking soda
260 g (2 cups) unbleached flour

1. Lightly grease cookie sheet. Heat oven to 177C (350F).
2. Beat together butter, peanut butter, demerara sugar, and yogurt, if desired, until light and fluffy with vanilla.
3. Sift all dry ingredients and stir into peanut butter mixture.
4. Chill until easily handled.
5. Roll dough in balls the size of large walnuts. Arrange on a cookie sheet about 7.5 cm (3 in.) apart. Dip a fork into flour and press it, first one way then the other, to flatten.
6. Bake in centre of oven until lightly browned (about 10-12 minutes). This makes about 24 cookies.

ROLLED COOKIES

For these cookies you need a rolling pin and cookie cutters. These are a bit more difficult than the others, becase you have to roll the dough. To make it easier you can chill the dough first.

Cut rolled cookies in different ways to make them interesting. Before baking you can spread the cookies with chopped nuts. After baking, different toppings may be added. Only bake cookies until lightly browned, otherwise they will be tough and dry.

OATMEAL COOKIES
(Non dairy)

120 g (1 cup) unbleached flour
7.5 mL (1/2 tbs.) baking soda
2.5 mL (1/2 tsp.) sea salt
100 g (1 cup) quick oats
315 g (1 1/2 cups) demerara sugar
125 mL (1/2 cup) unsalted butter (softened) or soft margarine
60 mL (1/4 cup) milk or water

1. Lightly grease cookie sheet. Heat oven to 177C (350F).
2. Mix dry ingredients.
3. Melt butter and add to dry ingredients. Add milk to form a moist dough.
4. Roll the dough, half of it at a time, from the centre to the edge until about .63 cm (1/4 in.) thick. Cut with a cookie cutter previously dipped in flour.
5. Place 2.5 cm (1 in.) apart on cookie sheet, bake in preheated oven until light brown (6-8 minutes). Makes about 2 dozen.

PLAIN COOKIES

150 mL (2/3 cup) unsalted butter, softened
150 g (3/4 cup) raw sugar
30 mL (2 tbs.) yogurt
5 mL (1 tsp.) vanilla
240 g (2 cups) unbleached flour
7.5 mL (1/2 tbs.) baking powder
1.2 mL (1/4 tsp.) sea salt
45 mL (3 tbs.) milk (approx.)

1. Grease cookie sheet. Heat oven to 191C (375F).
2. Beat until very light and fluffy, butter and sugar. Beat in yogurt and vanilla.
3. Sift together flour, baking powder and salt.
4. Stir dry ingredients into butter mixture adding milk to form a moist dough.
5. Roll dough from the centre out .63 cm (1/4 in.) thick, cut with cookie cutter first dipped in flour.
6. Place 2.5 cm (1/2 inch) apart on cookie sheet.
7. Bake on centre rack in preheated oven 8-9 minutes, or until light brown. This makes about 2 dozen cookies.

NO BAKE CAROB CANDY
(Non dairy)

250 mL (1 cup) hard honey
250 mL (1 cup) peanut butter
60-130 g (1/2 - 1 cup) roasted carob powder, sifted
160 g (1 cup) sesame seeds, lightly toasted
120 g (1 cup) shelled roasted sunflower seeds
50 g (1/2 cup) roasted medium unsweetened coconut
95 g (1/2 cup) chopped washed dates, apricots, or raisins

1. Grease one 20 cm (8 in.) square pan with unsalted butteror oil.
2. Thoroughly hand-mix all ingredients in a large bowl.
3. Spread in the pan and refrigerate until firm.

NO BAKE CAROB COOKIES
(Non dairy)

420 g (2 cups) raw sugar
125 mL (1/2 cup) milk
125 mL (1/2 cup) salted butter or soft margarine
32 g (1/4 cup) roasted carob powder
300 g (3 cups) instant rolled oats
5 mL (1 tsp.) vanilla
60 g (1/2 cup) walnut pieces
100 g (1 cup) roasted medium coconut

1. Combine first 4 ingredients in a thick bottomed sauce pan and bring to a boil over medium heat. Remove from heat and stir in everything else.
2. Drop by spoonfuls onto waxed paper. Chill until set. Makes two dozen.

MINUTE FUDGE

250 mL (1 cup) melted butter, unsalted
410 g (2 cups) demerara sugar
125 mL (1/2 cup) milk
260 g (2 cups) whole milk powder (skim causes lumps)
chopped walnuts to taste

1. Beat brown sugar into butter and bring to a full boil. Boil 2 minutes.
2. Add milk and bring to boil until sugar is dissolved.
3. Turn off heat and beat in remaining ingredients with a wire whisk.
4. Spread in a large pan, cool, then cut into squares.

CAROB FUDGE

1.2 kg (6 cups) raw or demerara sugar
500 mL (2 cups) milk
75 mL (1/3 cup) corn syrup
1.2 mL (1/4 tsp.) sea salt
175 mL (3/4 cup) unsalted butter
130 g (1 cup) roasted carob powder, sifted
mixed with 125 mL (1/2 cup) water
10 mL (2 tsp.) vanilla
(2 cups) crushed walnuts (opt.)

1. Grease a 23 cm (9 in.) x 33 cm (13 in.) baking pan with unsalted butter.
2. Combine everything but vanilla and nuts in a large thick bottomed pot.
3. Bring to a boil over a high heat, stirring constantly, when boiling reduce heat and boil slowly to 115C (239F) on candy thermometer or until it forms a soft ball when dripped into cold water. Do not stir when it boils.
4. Cool pan in a sink containing cold water to about 43C (110F) or until slightly thickened.
5. When ready, pour into a large bowl, add vanilla and beat until it loses most of its gloss. Stir in nuts, if desired, and scrape into the pan.

JELLO SUBSTITUTE
(Non dairy)

250 mL (1 cup) cool water
1 L (4 cups) non-citrus juice
90 mL (6 tbs.) agar flakes (approx.)
(available at health food stores)

1. Add agar flakes to water and bring to boil over medium heat, stirring constantly. When boiling, turn heat to simmer and let most of the flakes dissolve.
2. Pour fruit juice in a bowl, room temperature and strain the agar mixture into it. Stir well. Chill. It will be ready in a couple of hours. To make fruit jello: after about 30 minutes, or when jello is partially set, add your favourite cut fruit.

13

Wholesome Grains

YEAST BREADS
WHOLE WHEAT BREAD

250 mL (1 cup) milk, scalded
250 mL (1 cup) cold water
5 mL (1 tsp.) raw sugar
1 package fast rising dry yeast
   (15 mL (1tbs.) in bulk form)
10 mL (2 tsp.) sea salt
45mL (3 tbs.) molasses
30 mL (2 tbs.) unsalted butter, melted
325 g (2 1/2 cups) whole wheat flour
300 g (2 1/2 cups) unbleached flour or
   650 g (5 cups) chapati flour

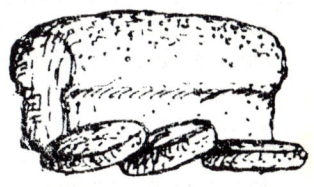

1. Scald milk and add water. Measure 1/2 cup of the liquid, add 5 mL (1 tsp.) of sugar and let cool to lukewarm. Sprinkle yeast over top and set in warm spot for 10 minutes. Add salt, butter and molasses to remaining liquid. Mix everything.
2. Add unbleached flour to large bowl. Mix in whole wheat flour .
3. Add half of the flour to liquid and beat until smooth (100 strokes).
4. Gradually stir in enough flour to make a soft dough.
5. Turn out on a lightly floured board and knead until dough is satiny and elastic, about 8-10 minutes.
6. Put dough in a lightly greased mixing bowl. Cover with greased, waxed paper and clean cloth. Let rise in warm place 24 to 29C (74-84 F) until doubled in volume (about 1 1/2 hours).
7. Punch down dough. Turn out on lightly greased board. Cut into two pieces with a greased sharp knife. Cover each piece with a towel and let sit 15 minutes.
8. With rolling pin, roll dough out to uniform thickness, stretching by hand to form rectangle approximately 23 cm x 30 cm (9x12 in.). Break all gas bubbles in the outer edge of the dough.
9. From far edge, roll dough toward you, jelly roll fashion, sealing dough with heal of hand after each roll. (About four turns will bring you to the last seal). Be sure to seal final seam on bottom of loaf.
10. Seal loaf ends by using the side of hand to get a thin sealed strip.
11. Using fingers, fold under sealed loaf ends. Avoid tearing dough.
12. Place shaped loaf, with seam side down, in a well greased bread pan approx. 20 cm x 12 cm (8 in. x 5 in.) top inside measure. Cover pans with greased waxed paper and clean cloth. Let rise in a warm place until doubled in volume (about 11/2 hours). If desired, brush top with a combination of milk, paprika, and toasted sesame seeds.
13. Bake in moderately hot oven, 205C (400F) for 45 minutes. Test for doneness by tapping to make sure top is hard, and has a somewhat hollow sound. The bottom should be brown and firm. Remove from pan and cool on rack.

QUICK BREAD

**300 g (2 1/2 cups) unbleached flour
or half whole wheat and half white
15 mL (1 tbs.) active dry yeast
2.5 mL (1/2 tsp.) sea salt
30 mL (2 tbs.) raw sugar
125 mL (1/2 cup) whole milk
30 mL (2 tbs.) butter, unsalted**

1. Combine 90 g (3/4 cups) flour with yeast, sugar and salt. At this point you may add various types of seeds, cheese or dried fruit, etc.
2. Add milk, butter and water to thick bottomed pot and heat until butter melts.
3. Mix liquids into flour mixture and beat well. Add flour to make a smooth dough. Let rise 20 minutes.
4. Use this dough to make buns and bread, or whatever you like.

WHITE FLOUR ROLLS

250 mL (1 cup) milk
70 g (1/3 cup) raw sugar
10 mL (2 tsp.) sea salt
90 mL (6 tbs.) unsalted butter, melted
10 mL (2 tsp.) raw sugar
125 mL (1/2 cup) lukewarm water
2 packages fast rising dry yeast or
    20 mL (4 tsp.) bulk yeast
420 g (3 1/2 cups) unbleached flour

1. Scald milk. Remove from stove and add 75 g (1/3 cup) sugar, salt and butter. Cool to lukewarm. Add to a large bowl.
2. Measure lukewarm water into bowl. Stir in 10 mL (2 tsp.) sugar, sprinkle yeast over top and allow to stand 10 minutes in a warm place.
3. Mix well.
4. Stir in lukewarm milk mixture.
5. Add 240 g (2 cups) flour and beat until smooth (about 100 strokes).
6. Work in gradually enough flour to make a soft dough that comes freely from the side of the bowl.
7. Turn out on a lightly greased surface. Knead until smooth and elastic, 8 minutes. Place in a greased bowl. Cover with greased waxed paper and let rise in a warm place 24 to 29C (74 to 84F) until doubled in volume (about 1 hour).
8. Cut dough in half. Roll each piece with palms of hands in cylindrical shapes about 50 cm (20 in.) long. With greased sharp knife cut each into 12 pieces of equal size. Roll pieces of dough into balls under palm of hand, pressing gently. Place balls almost touching in 2 greased 20 cm. (8 in.) layer pans. Brush with butter or milk with paprika added, sprinkle toasted sesame seeds on top.
9. Cover and let rise in a warm place 24-29C (74-84F) until doubled in volume (1 hour). Bake in moderately hot oven 191C (375F) for about 20 minutes. Turn out on wire rack to cool. Brush tops with melted butter.

VEGIBURGER BUNS

1. After letting dough rise for the first time, punch down and turn it out on a greased surface. Roll dough with palms of hands in 2 cylindrical shapes about 51 cm. (20 in. long). With a greased sharp knife cut rolls into 14 equal pieces. Roll pieces of dough into balls under palm of hand, pressing gently. Place rolls 5 cm. (2 in.) apart on greased baking sheets. Cover and let rise in a warm place 24 to 29C (74 to 84F) for 15 minutes. Flatten and let rise again until doubled in volume (about 1 hour).
2. Bake in a moderately hot oven 191C (375F) for about 20 minutes.
3. Brush tops with melted butter.

VARIATION

For whole wheat rolls and buns use the white flour rolls recipe. Use brown sugar for raw sugar and 1/2 whole wheat flour and 1/2 white flour.

BAKING POWDER BISCUITS

240 g (2 cups) unbleached flour
7.5 mL (1/2 tbs.) baking powder
3.6 mL (3/4 tsp.) sea salt
60 mL (4 tbs.) unsalted butter
175 mL (3/4 cup) milk

1. Preheat oven to 232C (450F).
2. Mix well, or sift together first 3 ingredients.
3. Cut in butter with a pastry blender or two knives. The mixture should look like course crumbs, or cornmeal. Make a "well" in the flour mixture.
4. Add all the milk to the "well" and stir with a fork until flour is dampened.
5. Gently knead the dough 5 or 6 times, this helps make the biscuits light and fluffy.
6. Pat with hands or roll out dough 1.2 cm. (1/2 in.) thick. Roll half as thick for crusty biscuits.
7. Cut biscuits out with lightly floured 5 cm. (2 in.) cutter, don't twist cutter- cut straight down.
8. Place circles 2.5 cm. (1 in.) apart on ungreased cookie sheet, if you prefer soft edges , place them closer together.
9. Place in centre of preheated oven, bake 10 to 12 minutes or until golden brown. This makes about 2 dozen.

VARIATIONS

1. For richer biscuits use an extra 30 mL (2 tbs.) butter and use 150 mL (2/3 cup) milk.
2. Make cheese biscuts by adding 175 mL (3/4 cup) grated sharp cheddar cheese to dry ingredients.
3. Make orange biscuits by adding grated peel of one orange to dry ingredients.
4. Cheese topped biscuits may be prepared by melting 85 grams (3 oz.) pimento cream cheese with 30 mL (2 tbs.) butter and adding to top of biscuits before baking.
5. Make peach biscuits by adding 250 mL (1 cup) chopped peaches and 5 mL (1 tsp.) orange rind and 30 mL (2 tbs) raw sugar.
6. Prepare cinnamon rolls by rolling biscuit dough cut about .3 cm. (1/8 in.) thick and about 38 cm. x 25 cm. (15 x 10 in.). Top with butter, then sprinkle with cinnamon, brown sugar and raisins. Roll up lengthwise, slice 1.9 cm. (3/4 in.) thick. Bake on a greased cookie sheet 12 min. at 205C (400F) or until browned. They should be a bit crunchy. Makes about 16.
7. A tea ring may be made by rolling out biscuit dough as for cinnamon rolls but instead top with jam. Roll up dough, form a circle, and bake at 205C (400F) for 25 minutes or until browned and a bit crunchy.

BRAN MUFFINS

150 g (1 1/2 cups) bran
130 g (1 cup) whole wheat flour
15 mL (1 tbs.) baking powder
5 mL (1 tsp.) baking soda
2.5 mL (1/2 tsp.) sea salt
105 g (1/2 cup) demerara sugar
75 g (1/2 cup) raisins
60 mL (4 tbs.) molasses
250 mL (1 cup) milk
60 mL (4 tbs.) melted unsalted butter

1. Preheat oven to 205C (400F). Grease bottoms of medium muffin cups with shortening.
2. Mix together all dry ingredients. Make a "well" in the centre.
3. Mix together well the last 3 ingredients. Pour as one into "well" in flour mixture.
4. Mix quickly and lightly with a fork until all the flour is moistened,   but do not beat. The batter will be lumpy.
5. Quickly fill greased muffin cups 2/3 full with batter. Wipe off any spilled batter.
6. Bake in preheated oven in centre rack about 15 minutes, or until muffins are golden. You may test with a cake tester or wooden picks, if it comes out clean muffins are done.
7. Remove. Run a spatula around the outside edge of each muffin to loosen, lift out. Makes 1 dozen.

MATHURA MUFFINS

180 g (1 1/2 cups) unbleached flour
15 mL (1 tbs.) baking powder
1.2 mL (1/4 tbs.) sea salt
30 mL (2 tbs.) raw sugar
30 mL (2 tbs.) yogurt
250 mL (1 cup) milk
60 mL (4 tbs.) melted, unsalted butter
5 mL (1 tsp.) vanilla

1. Preheat oven to 205C (400F). Grease bottoms of medium muffin cups with shortening.
2. Mix together well all dry ingredients, make a "well" in the centre.
3. Mix together well the last 3 ingredients. Pour as one into "well" in flour mixture.
4. Mix quickly and lightly with a fork until all the flour is moistened, but do not beat. The batter will be lumpy.
5. Quickly fill greased muffin cups 2/3 full with batter. Wipe off any spilled batter.
6. Bake in preheated oven in centre rack about 15 minutes, or until muffins are golden. You may test with a cake tester or wooden picks, if it comes out clean muffins are done.
7. Remove. Run a spatula around the outside edge of each muffin to loosen, lift out.

VARIATIONS

1. Blueberry muffins may be prepared by adding washed and drained blueberries, about 250 mL (1 cup), with last couple of strokes of mixing. You may also add instead 75 g (1/2 cup) raisins, finely chopped dates, or coconut with last couple of strokes of mixing.
2. Cheese muffins may be prepared by folding in 125 mL (1/2 cup) sharp cheese into batter, with the last few strokes of mixing.

DOUGHNUTS

420 g (3 1/2 cups) unbleached flour
30 mL (2 tbs.) baking powder
2.5 mL (1/2 tsp.) cinnamon
2.5 mL (1/2 tsp.) nutmeg
5 mL (1 tsp.) sea salt
45 mL (3 tbs.) softened unsalted butter
160 g (3/4 cup) raw sugar
60 mL (4 tbs.) yogurt
250 mL (1 cup) milk
honey
fresh ghee or light vegetable oil for deep frying

1. Sift together first 5 ingredients.
2. Cream butter with half of sugar.
3. Beat yogurt with the rest of the sugar, mix in butter mixture.
4. Add dry ingredients alternatively with milk to form a soft but not sticky dough.
5. Roll dough .95 cm.(3/8 in.) thick, on lightly greased board, cut with floured doughnut cutter.
6. Fry in fresh ghee, or oil at 191C (375F) or about medium temperature. Fry until golden brown, turn only once. Cook about 1- 2 minutes on each side.
7. Cool and top with a little honey.

FRITTERS

360 g (3 cups) unbleached flour
10 mL (2 tsp.) sea salt
a pinch of pepper (opp)
10 mL (2 tsp.) garam masala
10 mL (2 tsp.) coriander
10 mL (2 tsp.) cinnamon
10 mL (2 tsp.) nutmeg
5 mL (1 tsp.) ginger powder
10 mL (2 tsp.) cloves
10 mL (2 tsp.) allspice
30 mL (2 tbs.) raw sugar
375 mL (3 1/2 cups) milk (approx.)
fresh ghee or light vegetable oil
sweetener (opt.)

1. Combine all ingredients but ghee or oil to form a thick batter.
2. Dip favourite fruit in batter to coat.
3. Fry both sides in hot ghee or oil until golden brown.
4. Top with sweetner, if desired.

STRAWBERRY SHORTCAKE

1. Preheat oven to 232C (450F). Grease well with vegetable shortening two 2 cm. (8 in.) square cake pans.
2. Divide dumpling dough ,below, in two and pat into greased pans.
3. Bake in preheated oven 10-12 minutes, or until lightly browned.
4. Cool 10 minutes, remove from pans, cool fully and cover one layer with a generous layer of sweetened strawberries. Put other layer on top and add lots of whipping cream. If desired, use other fruit and/or yogurt or sour cream.

DUMPLINGS

270 g (2 1/4 cups) unbleached flour
20 mL (4 tsp.) baking powder
2.5 mL (1/2 tsp.) sea salt
30 mL (2 tbs.) raw sugar
60 mL (4 tbs.) unsalted butter
250 ml (1 cup milk)

1. Combine all dry ingredients. Cut in butter as on page 86.
2. Add milk in a sauce pan, heat until warm.
3. Make a "well" in dry ingredients, pour milk into "well". Toss lightly with a fork until liquid is absorbed.
4. Knead lightly 5 or 6 times. Roll into balls the size of a tablespoon. Drop lightly on a cooking vegetable preparation, leaving a good space between each dumpling. Cover and steam about 12 minutes.

PANCAKES

240 g (2 cups) unbleached flour or buckwheat flour
5 mL (1 tsp.) nutmeg
15 mL (1 tbs.) baking powder
25 ml (1/2 tsp.) sea salt
60 mL (4 tbs.) yogurt or sour cream
500 mL (2 cups) milk(approx.)
60 mL (4 tbs.) unsalted, melted butter

1. Set electric griddle or skillet to pancake temperature, or if using grill or frying pan, set to low heat.
2. Sift together flour, baking powder, nutmeg and salt into a medium bowl.
3. Beat together yogurt, milk and butter.
4. Make a "well" in centre of flour, pour in liquid, stir until wet flour mixture is lumpy.
5. When water dances when it hits the grill and forms little beads it is ready.
6. When grill is ready, drop batter from a 125 mL (1/2 cup) measure onto grill to make a pancake. Lightly spread pancake out with the back of measure.
7. Cook until the cakes are full of bubble holes, the edges are dry and the pancakes are golden underneath. Then turn with a pancake turner. Turn only once or they will be tough. Brown on the underside, This will take about 2 minutes.

(Delicious served with lots of whipped butter and maple syrup).

VARIATIONS

1. When batter is on the grill sprinkle on a few blueberries.
2. Wash an apple, core, peel and slice it, and stir into the batter, add a sprinkle of cinnamon.
3. Stir in 250 mL (1 cup) of your favorite roasted or chopped nuts.

BREAKFAST CEREALS

MILLET

Millet is referred to as the best of grains by nutritional experts. It is high in calcium, iron and protein.

72 g (3/4 cup) washed millet
1L (4 cups) milk
5 mL (1 tsp.) sea salt
30 mL (2 tbs.) fresh ghee or unsalted butter
15-20 mL (1-2 tbs.) honey, or a handful of dates

1. Heat oven to 93C (200F). Combine millet and milk in a thick bottomed pot with a tight fitting lid.
2. Heat mixture until it is just beginning to boil. Cover and place in the oven.
3. Leave in oven about 2 1/2 hours. Remove and stir in salt, honey and ghee or butter. You may add dried fruit or nuts, etc. to make it fancier.
    This method may be used for any of your favourite grains, but adjustment of liquid may be required.

MILLET IN A DOUBLE BOILER

Simply follow instructions for oven method but add everything to the top portion of a double boiler with a tight fitting lid, without bothering to heat mixture first. Cook until soft, about 2 hours.

CRUNCHY GRANOLA
(Non dairy)

260 g (2 cups) rolled oats
80 g (1/2 cup) sesame seeds
60 g (1/2 cup) sunflower seeds, shelled
60 mL (1/4 cup) melted honey (approx.)
60 mL (4 tbs.) ghee or melted unsalted butter or margarine
5 mL (1 tsp.) vanilla
75 g (1/2 cup) raisins

1. Combine first 3 ingredients. Stir in ghee, oil or margarine and vanilla.
2. Spread on a shallow pan and bake 163C (325F) for 40 minutes, or until dry and brown. Stir every 10 minutes. Remove and add honey and raisins.

    For variety, replace or supplement the sesame seeds, sunflower seeds, and raisins with wheat germ, coconut, chopped buckwheat, currants and dates.

14

Exotic

dishes & soups

VEGETABLE SOUP
(Non dairy)

6 medium tomatoes, washed and blended
   dilute with equal water
4 small zucchini, washed and sliced
2 carrots, washed and sliced
2 sticks of celery, washed and sliced
2 medium potatoes, peeled and cubed small
5 mL (1 tsp.) asafoetida
4 bay leaves
15 mL (1 tbs.) thyme
125 mL (1/2 cup) butter or soft margarine
black pepper to taste (opp)
60 mL (4 tbs.) lemon juice
15 mL (1 tbs.) sea salt or to taste (opp)
a little raw sugar to taste
10 mL (2 tsp.) oregano

1. Boil vegetables together with bay leaves, asafoetida and thyme.
2. When vegetables are soft, add water, if desired to make thinner.
3. Turn off heat and add remaining ingredients. Serves 6.

   For a variation with an Italian touch; break into small pieces 1/4 of (500 g) 1 lb. box of vermicelli, and boil with the vegetables.

CREAMY VEGETABLE SOUP

4 medium potatoes, peeled and cubed small
2 carrots washed and chopped
2 sticks of celery, washed and chopped small
a little sweetener to taste
260 g (1 cup) milk powder, (non-instant, non-fat)
15 mL (1 tbs.) coriander powder
10 mL (2 tsp.) cumin powder
15 mL (1 tbs.) fenugreek powder
5 mL (1 tsp.) turmeric powder
oregano to garnish
black pepper to taste (opp)
15 mL (1 tbs.) sea salt or to taste
60 mL (1/4 cup) unsalted butter, melted

1. Add potatoes to thick bottomed pot, cover with water, add powdered spices, stir then cover pot and boil until potatoes are soft, then mash well.
2. Add other vegetables and a little water to thin out potato. Cover pot and boil until vegetables are soft.
3. Turn off heat, mix milk powder with a little water to form a paste, stir in with remaining ingredients. Thin out soup for ease of service. Serves 6.

VARIATIONS

1. Stir 500 mL (2 cups) cream into soup instead of milk powder.
2. Instead of adding water to thin add 5 blended tomatoes with a little extra water.

CORN SOUP

Scrape corn off 4 ears of corn and add to 2L (8 cups) boiling milk. Boil for 10 minutes. Mix 60mL (1/4 cup) cornstarch with a little cold water and beat in to milk, stir until thickened. Turn off heat, sprinkle in a little cardamom powder and 10 mL (2 tsp.) salt, or to taste. This serves 6.
SPECIAL NOTE: Pressed curd may be cubed and deep fried and added to any soup. (see pg. 8).

SUPER SOUP
(Non dairy)

190 g (1 cup) soup mix, washed (readily availabe at markets)
1 carrot washed and chopped
1/2 potato medium sized, washed and cubed
1 stick celery, washed and chopped
3 medium tomatoes, washed and cubed
15 mL (1 tbs.) cumin powder
5 mL (1 tsp.) thyme
5 mL (1 tsp.) rosemary
15 mL (1 tbs.) dill weed
15 mL (1 tbs.) oregano
125 mL (1/2 cup) fresh ghee or unsalted butter or margarine
15 mL (1 tbs.) sea salt or to taste
juice of 1 lemon
a little sweetener

1. Boil soup mix, add water as needed. When soup mix begins to soften add vegetables, cumin, thyme, and rosemary. Boil until soup mix is soft and vegetables are cooked.
2. Turn off heat and add remaining ingredients. Cover and let steam 5-10 minutes. Serves 4 or 5.

ITALIAN COOKING
PIZZA DOUGH

30 mL (2 tbs.) yeast
125 mL (1/2 cup) warm water
15 mL (1 tbs.) demerara sugar
250 mL (1 cup) warm milk
30 mL (2 tbs.) melted unsalted butter
5 mL (1 tsp.) sea salt
240 g (2 cups) unbleached flour, sifted. (approx.)

1. Preheat oven to 177C (350F).
2. Put water in bowl, stir in sugar and sprinkle yeast. Let set until it bubbles.
3. Add warm milk, melted butter and salt.
4. Add 120 g (1 cup) of the flour and beat.
5. Wor k in more flour to make a soft dough.
6. Let rise for 20 minutes.
7. Divide dough and stretch into 2 or 3 30 cm. (12 in.) pizza pans depending on thickness of crust desired.
8. Bake on middle rack of oven until dough is browned on bottom, about 10 minutes.

SAUCE AND TOPPING

5 L (20 cups) washed and blended tomatoes
60 mL (4 tbs.) paprika
250 mL (1 cup) extra virgin olive oil
52 g (1/4 cup) raw sugar (approx.)
2 small tins tomato paste
60 mL (4 tbs.) coriander
15 mL (1 tbs.) oregano
sprinkle of basil leaves
20 mL (4 tsp.) sea salt or to taste
3 medium green peppers, washed and cubed,
     removing white portion
1 large eggplant, washed and cubed very small
2 390 mL (14 oz.) tins black olives chopped
one large tin of pineapple nibblets (drained) (opp.)
910 g (2 tbs.) grated mozzarella cheese (approx.)
ghee or olive oil for deep frying

1. Cook down slowly in a thick bottomed pot first 6 ingredients.
2. When sauce is thick add next 3 ingredients, stir well, then turn off heat.
3. Heat gee or oil until very hot, deep fry green peppers until soft, and drain.
4. Deep fry eggplant until soft in hot gee or oil and drain well.
5. Arrange pizza by spreading tomato sauce evenly over cooked crust.
6. Spread green peppers evenly over top, along with eggplant and black olives and pineapple if desired.
7. Top with the cheese.
8. Bake at 177C (350F) until the cheese is melted, about 30 minutes, cool before serving. Serves 8 or 9.

INSTANT PIZZA

To the browned crust pour on a layer of blended tomatoes, that have been cooked down. Sprinkle with olive oil and oregano. Grate mozzarella cheese on top to your desired amount and bake in a hot oven until the cheese melts.

SPAGHETTI

1. Boil one 500 g (1 lb.) pkg. of spaghetti according to package directions. Rinse well to remove exces starch.
2. Follow exactly steps 1-4 in pizza recipe except prepare 1/2 of recipe. Stir eggplant, peppers and olives into the sauce. Serve by putting spaghetti on plate and putting sauce on top. Keep spaghetti in cool water until used so it won't stick together, or add olive oil, mixing well.
3. Add barra, kofta balls or pressed and cubed curd deep fried. (see index). Serves 6.

MACARONI

1. Boil 500 g (1 lb.) of macaroni according to package directions. Rinse well to remove excess starch, or add butter or olive oil so it isn't sticky.
2. Follow exactly steps 1-4 in pizza recipe (except prepare 1/2 of recipe). Stir eggplant, peppers and olives into sauce.
3. Stir together macaroni and sauce and add to a large casserole dish. Grate 454 g (1 lb.) mozzarella cheese and spread on top.
4. Bake 177C (350F) for aobut 30 minutes. Serves 4 or 5.

LASAGNA

SAUCE

Prepare a pizza sauce, except prepare 1/2 of recipe.

CURD

Follow process for making curd on page 8, but don't press, using 4 L (1 gal.) milk. Just before curdling add 30 mL (2 tbs.) oregano.

NOODLES

Boil lasagna noodles according to package instructions. Drain and rinse under cold water.

ARRANGEMENT

1. Heat oven to 177C (350F).
2. Spread 1/3 of the sauce on bottom of a 23 cm. x 35 cm. (9 in. x 14 in.) pan. Spread 1/2 of the curd evenly on top of sauce, crumbling it into little pieces. Then add 1/2 of the noodles, then 1/2 of remaining sauce and spread evenly. Crumble remaining curd and spread evenly over sauce. Spread evenly remaining noodles, then the rest of the sauce.
3. Grate 454 g (1 lb.) mozzarella cheese and spread on top.
4. Bake about 30 minutes. Serve warm. Serves 8.

EGGPLANT PARMESAN

SAUCE

Prepare the sauce as you do for lasagna (on previous page).

PAKORAS

120 g (1 cup) unbleached flour
150 g (1 1/2 cups) sifted chickpea flour
7.5 ml (1/2 tsp.) sea salt
10 ml (2 tsp.) coriander
10 ml (2 tsp.) asafoetida
10 ml (2 tsp.) paprika
1 medium eggplant. (Wash, cut in half, then slice halves in 1.2 cm (1 in) pieces.
ghee or olive oil for deep frying

1. Mix well all spices with flour and add water to form a thin batter.
2. Heat ghee or oil until almost smoking, dip eggplant in batter so it is thinly coated. Deep fry until eggplant is soft and batter is crisp. Remove and drain.

CURD

Follow process for making curd (see page 8), without pressing. Use 4L (1 gal.) milk, and just before curdling, add 30 ml (2 tbs.) oregano.

CHEESE

Grate 454 g (1 lb.) parmesan cheese.

PREPARATION INSTRUCTIONS

1. Preheat oven to 177C (350F).
2. Spread 1/3 of sauce on botom of 23 cm., 35 cm (9 in. x 14 in.) pan.
3. Add 1/2 of eggplant pakoras, covering sauce evenly.
4. Add all of the pressed curd, breaking it up and spreading it evenly over the top.
5. Add 1/2 remaining sauce, spreading it evenly over curd.
6. Add remaining pakoras eveniy over sauce.
7. Spread remainder of sauce evenly over pakoras.
8. Spread grated cheese evenly over sauce.
9. Bake about 30 minutes. Serve warm. (Serves 4 or 5).

ITALIAN SALAD
(Suggested ingredients)

Salad macaroni, boiled until soft with butter or olive oil added so it's not sticky
chopped avacadoes, alfalfa sprouts
cubed tofu, grated or cubed mozzarella cheese
lettuce (torn), peas, sliced tomatoes, sunflower seeds, raisins
extra virgin olive oil, plus sea salt, pepper, and basil to taste

Use these ingredients and your own imagination to suit your personal taste. Macaroni should equal total bulk of other items.

UKRANIAN COOKING

CABBAGE ROLLS

FILLING

140 g (2 cups) washed basmati or regular rice
500 mL (2 cups) water
125 mL (1/2 cup) butter, unsalted
5 mL (1 tsp.) asafoetida
10 mL (2 tsp.) sea salt or to taste
1 medium eggplant cubed small
2 sticks celery, chopped small
ghee or light vegetable oil for deep frying

1. Add rice to rapidly boiling water, let cook 1 minute. Cover, turn off heat and let stand until water is absorbed.
2. Fry asafoetida in butter until lightly toasted and add rice with salt.
3. Deep fry eggplant until soft, drain well and stir into rice with celery.

VARIATIONS

1. Use milk instead of water.
2. Use half water, half tomato juice.

SAUCE

Blend 10 tomatoes and add 2 small tins of tomato paste. Stir in 5 mL (1 tsp.) asafoetida, 15 mL (1 tbs.) coriander powder, black pepper to taste, 30 mL (2 tbs.) raw sugar, 125 mL (1/2 cup) butter, 500 mL (2 cups) yogurt or sour cream and 5 mL (1 tsp.) salt or to taste.

CABBAGE PREPARATION

1. Remove core from cabbage by cutting around with a sharp knife.
2. Place whole cabbage head in a pot, add water to cover head completely. Boil until leaves are soft.
3. Drain and take leaves off carefully, don't tear them. Remove hard rib from each leaf. Trim leaves so they are about 10 cm. (4 in.) in diameter.

ROLLING AND COOKING

1. Cover half of cabbage with filling and roll up carefully put seam side down in a 23 cm. x 35 cm. (9 in. x 14 in.) pan. After bottom is covered pour on half the sauce. Place remaining cabbage rolls on top in other direction, and add rest of the sauce, evenly over top. Put on tight fitting lid.
2. Bake in a 177C (350F) oven for about 2 hours. Serve hot. Serves 4 to 6.

BORSTCH

1000 ML (4 cups) tomatoes, chopped
125 ML (1/2 cup) butter
8 medium potatoes scrubbed and cut in 2.5 cm. (1 in.) cubes
1 carrot washed and cubed
1 stalk celery, washed and chopped
1 green pepper washed cut in half and chopped (white portion
**   removed)**
1 medium head of cabbage washed and shredded
1 medium beet washed and cubed
250 ML (1 cup) cream
small bunch of dill leaves
salt to taste

1. Add tomatoes, 1/2 of butter, potatoes, carrot and celery to 3 L (3 quarts) boiling water.
2. Fry remaining ingredients in remaining butter until soft.
3. Combine all ingredients.

CHINESE COOKING

TOFU VEGETABLE
(Non dairy)

125 mL (1/2 cup) ghee or peanut oil
2 stalks celery washed and chopped very small
5 mL (1 tsp.) asafoetida
10 mL (2 tsp.) fenugreek powder
2.5 cm. (1 in.) square piece ginger root, minced
10 mL (2 tsp.) red miso mixed with water to form a thick paste
125 mL (1/2 cup) lemon juice
125 mL (1/2 cup) honey
8 tomatoes, washed with 5 blended and 3 chopped
500 mL (2 cups) cubed tofu
1 tin sweetened pineapple tidbits
sea salt to taste
35 g (1/3 cup) cornstarch mixed with
60 mL (4 tbs.) water to form a paste

1. Heat half the gee or oil and add tofu; lightly brown tofu.
2. Add the rest of the gee or oil to a thick bottomed pot, along with asafoetida, fenugreek and celery. Fry about 2 minutes then add ginger root and fry until browned.
3. Stir in all remaining ingredients except cornstarch and cook slowly on medium to low heat stirring occasionally.
4. Cook for 15 minutes covered, then stir in cornstarch paste and cook until thickened. Serves 6 or 7.

ALMOND CHOP SUEY
(Non dairy)

90 mL (6 tbs.) peanut oil or ghee (approx.)
3 stalks celery, washed and cut diagonally in bite-size peices
one large green pepper, washed, cut in half, white part
    removed and cut diagonally in bite-sized pieces
1 L (4 cups) washed mung sprouts
500 mL (2 cups) washed shredded cabbage
soya sauce to taste
5 mL (1 tsp.) anise powder
10 mL (2 tsp.) Chinese 5 kinds of spice
5 mL (1 tsp.) coriander powder
roasted almonds

1. Heat one-half gee or oil in wok or thick bottomed pot until it begins to smoke, and stir in celery and green pepper and fry stirring constantly until soft, but still crisp. Remove with a slotted spoon.
2. Heat remaining gee or oil until it smokes and add sprouts, cabbage and spices. Fry over high heat striiring often until sprouts are a bit translucent. Turn off heat, add other vegetables and stir in almonds and soya sauce. To make it more authentic, chop up a tin of bamboo shoots and add a tin of water chestnuts with a little extra soya sauce. Cubed pressed curd is also very good in this (see page 8). Serves 4 or 5.

Note: Chop suey is best served right after cooking. Letting it sit anytime before serving tends to make it become soggy.

SPRING ROLLS
DOUGH
(Non dairy)
260 g (2 cups) sifted chapati flour or
1/2 whole wheat/ 1/2 unbleached flour
125ml (1/2 cup) butter or soft margarine
125 mL (1/2 cup) cold water (approx.)

1. Break butter into flour and mix in until evenly dispersed.
2. Add water to form a stiff dough and knead until smooth.

FILLING

625 mL (2 1/2 cups) washed mung sprouts
625 mL (2 1/2 cups) washed shredded cabbage
250 mL(1 cup) washed peas
5 mL (1 tsp.) anise powder
10 mL (2 tsp.) chinese 5 kinds spice
90 mL (6 tbs.) ghee or peanut oil
soya sauce to taste
cubed ginger root to taste (opt.)
ghee or peanut oil for deep frying

1. Heat gee or oil until it smokes then add sprouts, cabbage, ginger root, and spices. Fry briefly stirring constantly until soft but still a bit crisp.
2. Turn off heat, stir in peas and soya sauce.

PREPARATION

1. Divide dough into 20 equal balls and roll out thinly as close to a rectangle as possible. Trim edges to make an exact rectangle shape. With extra dough roll out and trim the same way.
2. Place a generous amount of filling in centre of each rectangle.
3. Fold one edge of dough over filling lengthwise, wet other edge of dough and fold over on top of dough, seal edge - press ends to seal well. It should be cigar shaped and tightly packed with filling.
4. Heat ghee or oil until just below smoking point and fry until brown on both sides. Excellent served with a plum sauce.

TEMPURA

260 g (2 cups) whole wheat flour
10 mL (2 tsp.) sea salt
65 g (1/2 cup) non-instant, non-fat dry milk powder
15 mL (1 tbs.) baking powder
50 g (1/2 cup) wheat germ or bran
250 mL (1 cup) water (approx.)
ghee for deep frying or peanut oil

Combine all ingredients to form a thick batter. Heat ghee or oil but not to smoking. Cut up vegetables of your choice in bite-size pieces, avoiding vegetables with a high water content. Dip in batter and fry until golden brown on both sides and vegetable is cooked. For harder vegetables steam them first. Delicious served with the plum sauce.

PLUM SAUCE
(Non dairy)

1 small squash peeled and cubed
750 mL (3 cups) water
750 mL (3 cups) plums, pitted
110 g (1 cup) raw sugar
5 mL (1 tsp.) Chinese 5 kind spice
2.5 mL (1/2 tsp.) ginger powder
125 mL (1/2 cup) unsalted butter or soft margarine
5 mL (1 tsp.) sea salt or to taste
45 mL (3 tbs.) lemon juice

1. Boil squash uncovered until a bit soft over medium heat then add plums and everything but lemon juice and salt.
2. Boil, stirring occasionally until mixture is thick and smooth, mash if necessary. Add lemon juice and salt. Serve at room temperature or cold.

CHINESE 10 VEGETABLE SOUP
(Non dairy)

Cook down 10 different vegetables, mash and add water to make a thin soup. Spice to taste with Chinese spice (purchased at specialty shops), coriander powder, soya sauce, and a little raw sugar. Add peanut oil or unsalted butter to taste.

WONTON SOUP
(Non dairy)

1. Break up 1/4 of a 500 g (1 lb.) box of vermicelli into 5 cm. (2 in.) pieces and add to 2L (8 cups) of boiling water, add 60-125 mL (1/4 - 1/2 cup) soya sauce. Boil until tender, add 500 mL (2 cups) peas, boil briefly and turn off heat.
2. Fry 500 mL (2 cups) tofu cut in small cubes in 60 mL (1/4 cup) ghee or peanut oil over high heat with 5 mL (1 tsp.) asfoetida and 5 mL (1 tsp.) turmeric until lightly browned, stir into soup.
   Serves 6.

MEXICAN COOKING

TORTILLAS

Purchase tortilla shells in large supermarkets. Check ingredients carefully for animal products.

Peanut Filling

Add 150 g (1 1/2 cups) salted, roasted peanuts to blender with 45 mL (3 tbs.) lemon juice and an equal portion of water and salad oil. Blend, using a rubber spatula to work nuts to blade. It doesn't have to be completely smooth.

Guacamole

Mash 4 medium avacadoes with 5 mL (1 tsp.) asafoetida, 10 mL (2 tsp.) corriander, 2.5 mL (1/2 tsp.) chillie powder (or to taste) 250 mL (1 cup) sour cream, and 5 mL (1 tsp.) salt, or to taste. Make sure it is completely smooth.

Hot Sauce

Follow exactly recipe for hot sauce below. Now grate about 250 mL (1 cup) cabbage, red if possible, and 454 (1 lb.) jalapeño jack cheese. Chop 1 398 mL (14 oz.) tin of olives.

Assembly

In the shells add a layer of peanut filling, a layer of guacamole, some hot sauce, then a layer of cabbage, cheese and olives. Serves 4.

NATCHOS

Purchase corn chips at any grocery store. Check carefully for animal products.

HOT SAUCE

2 1/2 tomatoes washed and blended
half a small tin of tomato paste
7.5 mL (1/2 tbs.) oregano
7.5 mL (1/2 tbs.) coriander
7.5 mL (1/2 tbs.) cumin powder
5 mL (1 tsp) asafoetida
7.5 mL (1/2 tbs.) chilli powder (or to taste)
2.5 mL (1/2 tsp.) salt

TOPPING

Grate about 454 g (1 lb.) jalapeño jack cheese.

PREPARATION

1. Heat oven to 177C (350F).
2. Place chips on cookie sheet, then place a heaping 15 mL (1 tbs.) of refried beans on top (see bottom of next page). Cover with hot sauce, guacamole (prepared as for tortillas), then add cheese.
3. Bake until cheese melts.

SPANISH RICE

140 g (2 cups) basmati or plain rice, washed
1 L (4 cups) water
7.5 mL (1/2 tbs.) sea salt
125 mL (1/2 cup) butter, unsalted
500 mL (2 cups) carrots, washed and grated
2 green peppers, washed, cut in half, white portion removed and cut small
60 mL (4 tbs.) ghee or light vegetable oil
5 mL (1 tsp.) asafoetida
750 mL (3 cups) washed, blended tomatoes
1 small tin tomato paste
5 mL (1 tsp.) salt
30 mL (2 tbs.) raw sugar or to taste
Chilli powder to taste
454 g (1 lb.) grated jalapeño jack cheese

1. Add water, salt, butter and rice to a pot with tight fitting lid. Bring to a boil over high heat, stirring once or twice. When at a rapid boil, put on lid, reduce heat to low, and cook 20 minutes. Turn off heat and steam 20 minutes.
2. When rice is cooked scrape off in layers into a large casserole.
3. Heat ghee or oil in sauce pan until hot and add asafoetida. Toast until a bit brown, add carrots and green peppers. Fry briefly until vegetables are a bit soft.
4. Turn off heat and stir tomatoes, paste, salt, sugar and cayenne into rice.
5. Flatten top and spread grated cheese evenly over the top.
6. Bake in a 177C (350F) oven for 15 minutes or until cheese is melted. Serves 10.

MEXICAN SALAD
(Non dairy)

500 mL (2 cups) corn lightly steamed until soft, or canned
corn niblets, water drained
1 large red pepper (white part removed), washed & finely
chopped
1 large green pepper, prepared as for red pepper
30 mL (2 tbs.) parsley
5 mL (1 tsp.) salt (or to taste)
5 mL (1 tsp.) raw sugar
30 mL (1 tbs.) light vegetable oil or ghee
30 mL (2 tbs.) lemon juice
5 mL (1 tsp.) paprika

Combine all ingredients together and sprinkle paprika on top.

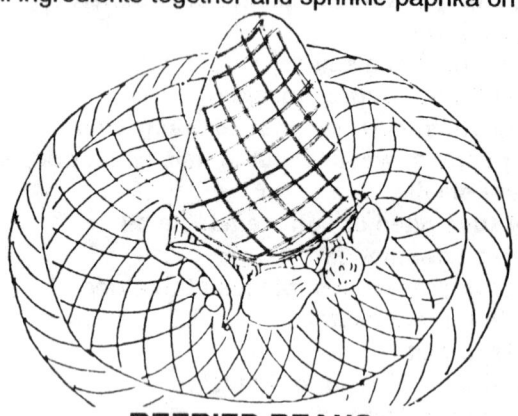

REFRIED BEANS

200 g (1 cup) pinto beans, washed and boiled until soft, with
    water boiled off
8 tomatoes washed, blended and cooked until thick
5 mL (1 tsp.) asafoetida
5 mL (1 tsp.) chilli powder to taste
5 mL (1 tsp.) oregano
10 mL (2 tsp.) salt (or to taste)
5 mL. (1 tsp.) raw sugar
50 mL (4 tbs.) ghee or light vegetable oil

Heat ghee or oil until it just begins to smoke and add cayenne and
asafoetida. Add cooked beans, fry over medium heat stirring constantly for a few minutes, then mash to a paste. Turn off heat and stir
in other ingredients.

CHILI NON CARNE
(Non dairy)

400 g (2 cups) kidney beans, washed and soaked overnight
2 or 3 bay leaves
12 tomatoes washed and blended
One handful texturized vegetable protein (also known as TVP-
- available at most health food stores)
250 mL (1 cup) butter or soft margarine
1 small tin tomato paste
5 mL (1 tsp.) cumin powder
60 mL (4 tbs.) ghee or light vegetable oil
5 mL (1 tsp.) chilli powder (or to taste)
5 mL (1 tsp.) asafoetida
30 mL (2 tbs.) demerara sugar
10 mL (2 tsp.) sea salt to taste

1. Boil beans in water they soaked in, with bay leaves and TVP, until they are soft. Add water if needed. When the beans are soft, boil off the excess water.
2. While beans are boiling, combine tomatoes with peppers,   butter, tomato paste and cumin powder.
3. Heat ghee or oil until just smoking in a large thick bottomed pot and add chilli powder and asafoetida. When the spices get a little brown, add tomato mixture and cook down uncovered over medium heat until thick.
4. When beans are soft, water is boiled off and tomato sauce has thickened up, combine the two and stir in sweetener and salt. Serves 6 to 8.

AMERICAN STYLE COOKING
HASH BROWNS
(Non dairy)

4 medium potatoes, scrubbed and grated, with excess water
**   wrung out.**
5 mL (1 tsp.) sea salt (or to taste)
5 mL (1 tsp.) asafoetida
pepper to taste
ghee or light vegetable oil for frying

Heat grill to about medium heat. Mix together spices and potatoes. Form in thin patties, fry on grill to which a little oil or ghee has been added until soft and well browned on both sides. If they are browned well but still not soft then cover with a large bowl and steam. This serves 4.

THE VEGIBURGER
(Non dairy)

225 g (2 cups) whole mung beans washed and soaked
24 hours
125 mL (1/2 cup) each, grated carrots, beets and celery
wringing out all the excess water
125 mL (1/2 cup) fresh melted ghee, butter or oil
7.5 mL (1/2 tbs.) sea salt or to taste
5 mL (1 tsp.) asafoetida
10 mL (2 tsp.) savory
15 mL (1 tbs.) paprika
ghee or light vegetable oil for frying
10-12 slices mild cheddar cheese (opp)

1. Blend beans, using as little water as possible. Use a rubber spatula to work beans into blade.
2. Remove blended beans and stir in vegetables, melted ghee or butter and all spices.
3. Heat frying pan or grill to medium heat and add layer of ghee or oil to pan.
4. Scoop out batter with 125 mL (1/2 cup) measure and spread on pan to form a patty.
5. Fry until brown, turn over and fry other side until brown. While frying other side top burger with a slice of cheese if desired.

MUSTARD
(Non dairy)

60 mL (4 tbs.) mustard powder
45 mL (3 tbs.) water
10 mL (2 tsp.) lemon juice
10 mL (2 tsp.) raw sugar
sea salt
30 mL (2 tbs.) chickpea flour

Simply mix to form a smooth paste.

VEGIBURGER SAUCE
(Non dairy)

398 mL (14 oz.) tin tomato sauce
30 mL (2 tbs.) sea salt
200 g (1 cup) raw sugar
30 mL (2 tbs.) lemon juice
5 mL (1 tsp.) asafoetida
30 mL (2 tbs.) coriander

Simply stir together well all ingredients. For chili sauce add 5 mL (1 tsp.) chili.

RELISH
(Non dairy)

250 mL (1 cup) very finely chopped green peppers
250 mL (1 cup) finely chopped peeled cucumber
500 mL (2 cups) water
1.2 mL (1/4 tsp.) black pepper
2.5 mL (1/2 tsp.) tumeric
1.2 mL (1/4 tsp.) cloves
1.2 mL (1/4 tsp.) coriander powder
4 bay leaves
2.5 mL (1/2 tsp.) sea salt
7.5 mL (1/2 tbs.) cornstarch
30 mL (2 tbs.) lemon juice

1. Boil together everything but last 3 ingredients over medium heat uncovered.
2. When only a little water remains mix together cornstarch with a little cold water and stir in to thicken up remaining water. Turn off heat and add salt and lemon juice.

MAYONNAISE
(Non dairy)

750 mL (3 cups) cubed tofu
30 mL (2 tbs.) lemon juice or to taste
30 mL (2 tbs.) light vegetable oil
7.5 mL (1/2 tbs.) basil
5 mL (1 tsp.) asafoetida
5 mL (1 tsp.) sea salt

Add everything to blender and blend until smooth.

VEGIBUTTER

Warm butter oe margarine to room temperature and stir in a little dill weed or parsley to taste. Add a little lemon juice and asafoetida to taste.

VEGIBURGER CONSTRUCTION

1. Prepare vegiburger buns as on page 104, and slice in half.
2. On the bun bottom spread a little mustard, go easy as it is strong.
3. On top of the mustard spread some mayonnaise.
4. Add burger with melted cheese on top.
5. Next add a layer of relish.
6. Add a layer of vegiburger sauce.
7. Add some sprouts or lettuce.
8. And to top it all off add the vegibutter on the top, then the other half of bun.

POTATO SALAD

4 medium potatoes, scrubbed and cubed
250 mL (1 cup) light vegetable oil
45 mL (3 tbs.) lemon juice
1.2 mL (1/4 tsp.) each, parsley, basil and sea salt
a sprinkle of finely chopped chives
one batch of mayonnaise (see above recipe)

1. Steam potatoes, be careful not to overcook.
2. Marinade potatoes in oil, lemon juice, parsley, basil and salt for a few hours, stirring now and again.
3. Drain off excess liquid and add chives and vegiburger mayonnaise to taste.

BRITISH SHEPHERDS' PIE

95 g (1 cup) washed basmati rice
125 mL (1/2 cup) butter
500 mL (2 cups) water
5 mL (1 tsp.) asafoetida

Combine all ingredients in a sauce pan with a tight fitting lid. Bring to a boil over medium heat. Cover, reduce heat to low and cook 25 minutes. After cooking fluff up with a fork.

POTATO TOPPING

5 medium potatoes scrubbed and cubed
250 mL (1 cup) milk
125 mL (1/2 cup) unsalted butter
5 mL (1 tsp.) pepper or cayanne
15 mL (1 tbs.) coriander powder
15 mL (1 tbs.) sea salt or to taste

Steam potatoes until soft. Mash well, stirring in all ingredients, beat until fluffy.

OTHER INGREDIENTS

1 batch pressed curd (see pg. 8)
750 mL (3 cups) corn
369 mL (13 oz.) tin tomato paste
10 mL (2 tsp.) savory
a sprinkle of raw sugar (opt.)
15 mL (1 tbs.) sea salt or to taste
454 g (16 oz.) grated mild cheddar cheese
a few sliced tomatoes

ASSEMBLY

1. Combine cooked rice with corn, pressed curd, tomato paste, savory, sugar and salt.
2. Spread evenly on bottom of a large casserole.
3. Spread potato topping evenly over top.
4. Top with sliced tomatoes and grated cheese.
5. Bake for 30 minutes in a 205C (400F) oven.

VARIATION

To make it fancier crumble up pressed curd and deep fry in hot ghee or oil until lightly browned. Served 8 to 10.

FRENCH CANADIAN PEA SOUP
(Non dairy)

235 g (1 1/4 cups) washed yellow soup peas
1.5 L (6 cups) water
2 carrots, scrubbed and chopped small
1 small turnip, peeled and cubed
2 stalks celery, washed and chopped small
5 mL (1 tsp.) asafoetida
15 mL (1 tbs.) sea salt or to taste
a sprinkle of savory
black pepper to taste
sweetner to taste
125 mL (1/2 cup) fresh ghee or unsalted butter or
    soft margarine

Combine all ingredients in a thick bottomed pot with the water and boil about 3 hours stirring occasionally, adding water as needed. The final product is thick. When finished cooking stir in salt. Serves 6.

FRENCH CANADIAN CASSEROLE

200 g (2 cups) chick peas, soak them overnight, boil them,
    boiling off excess water
500 ML (2 cups) diced tomatoes
500 ML (2 cups) shredded spinach
250 ML (1 cup) yogurt or sour cream
5 ML (1 tsp.) asafoetida
black pepper to taste
30 ML (2 tbs) coriander
10 ML (2tsp) turmeric
one basic white sauce recipe (see page 20) using chick pea
    flour
225 g (1/2 lb.) mild cheese grated

1. Preheat oven to 205 C (450 F)
2. Combine together ever thing except white sauce and cheese.
3. Spread 1/3 of chick pea mixture on the bottom of a casserole. Next add 1/2 of white sauce, then 1/2 of remaining chick pea mixture, then the rest of the sauce. Top with remaining chick pea mixture.
4. Bake about one half hour. Remove from oven and add cheese. Continue baking until cheese is melted. Cool before serving.

A MIDDLE EASTERN SALAD
(Non dairy)

155 g (1 cup) bulgar wheat soaked until soft and drained
250 mL (1 cup) chopped chives
1 green pepper, washed, cut in half with white portion
removed and chopped fine
110 g (1/2 cup) dried chickpeas soaked overnight and
cooked until soft, cook off excess water
4 tomatoes washed and chopped small
2 carrots, scrubbed and sliced paper thin
125 mL (1/2 cup) mashed tofu
60 mL (4 tbs.) light vegettable oil or butter
60 mL (4 tbs.) lemon juice
30-45 mL (2-3 tbs.) each parsley and tamari (available in
speciality shops)
7.5 mL (1/2 tbs.) sea salt or to taste
5 mL (1 tsp.) each basil, paprika, and oregano
1.2 mL (1/4 tsp.) each thyme and kelp powder
cayenne to taste

Mix together well, oil, lemon juice, all herbs and spices. In a separate bowl mix together all remaining ingredients. Combine everything and chill 1-2 hours. Stir every half hour. Serves 6.

YOGI SANDWICH

A half a batch of chapatis as on page 44
A batch of guacamole as on page 124
454 g (16 oz.) mild cheddar cheese
4 or 5 tomatoes washed and chopped
alphalpha sprouts to taste
pepper to taste

1. Heat oven to 218C (425F).
2. Fold chapatis in half.
3. Spread guacamole on top, then tomato wedges and cheese.
4. Bake until cheese melts.
5. Top with sprouts and salt and pepper.
6. Fold other half of chapati on the top.

"HAPPY FISH" SANDWICH SPREAD
(Non dairy) (The fish is happy because it is still in the water)

220 g (1 cup) dried chickpeas, washed and soaked overnight
250 mL (1 cup) finely chopped celery
15 mL (1 tbs.) finely chopped sweet pickles
30 mL (1 tbs.) sweet pickle juice
180 mL (3/4 cup) eggless mayonnaise
(available at health food stores)
2.5 mL (1/2 tsp.) paprika
a pinch of asafoetida
sea salt and pepper to taste
15 mL (1 tbs.) prepared mustard (opt.)

1. Boil chickpeas until soft then boil off excess water.
2. Mash chickpeas using as little water as possible.
3. Stir in all remaining ingredients.

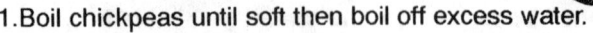

GLUTEN

The gluten protein content of whole wheat flour can be isolated by simple kneading, and then flavored in different ways to create meat taste. This is an inexpensive, cholesterol free, low calorie substitute for meat.

RAW GLUTEN PREPARATION
(Non dairy)

1.3 Kg (9 cups) whole wheat flour
750 mL (3 cups) warm water (approx.)
cold water for soaking
cold water for washing dough

1. Add enough water to flour to form into a stiff dough. Knead well.
2. Form dough into a ball, put in a bowl and cover.
3. Let soak for no less then 20 minutes and no more than 4 hours.
4. Knead dough in water carefully. The starch bran and wheat germ will come out in water, thus making water milky. Pour into container. Don't lose any of the solid dough. Continue washing until water is clear. If water is not completely clear the gluten will, when prepared, be doughy rather than chewy.

If you are not going to use gluten right away, soak it and store in a refrigerator. Oherwise it will become rubbery. The liquid is also nutritioun packed and can be added to any number of preparations, such as soups or cereals.

MOCK STEAK
(Non dairy)

5^0 mL (2 cups) raw glutten (approx.)
2 L (8 cups) water
60 mL (1/4 cup) tamari soya sauce
2.5 mL (1/2 tsp.) black pepper
60 mL (1/4 cup) fresh ghee or light vegetable oil
15 mL (1 tbs.) cumin powder
15 mL (1 tbs.) coriander powder
5 mL (1 tsp.) asafoetida

1. Divide raw gluten into 5 pieces and pound them into steak sized pieces.
2. Combine everything else in a pot and add steaks.
3. Cook over medium heat for 60 minutes, uncovered, without boiling rapily. The slow cooking lets the seasonings reach into the gluten. If steaks are spongy it means they were boiling too long or at too high a temperature.
4. After well draining steaks of all liquid, fry these in some ghee or oil on both sides while sprinkling various herbs and spices such as paprika, basil, asafoetida, pepper, thyme and salt. Use these in other recipes in this book.

MOCK CHICKEN
(Non dairy)

500 mL (2 cups) raw gluten
2 L (8 cups) water
15 mL (1 tbs.) nutritional yeast
2.5 mL (1/2 tsp.) sea salt
2.5 mL (1/2 tsp.) celery seed
1.2 mL (1/4 tsp.) sage
1.2 mL (1/4 tsp.) thyme
2.5 mL (1/2 tsp.) cumin powder
2.5 mL (1/2 tsp.) coriander powder
2.5 mL (1/2 tsp.) asafoetida
1.2 mL (1/4 tsp.) tarragon
1.2 mL (1/4 tsp.) rosemary
2.5 mL (1/2 tsp.) turmeric
15 mL (1 tbs.) corn oil

1. Divide gluten into 8 pieces and pound into oval shape (approx. 5 to 8 cm (2 -3 in.) wide.
2. Combine all other ingredients to form a broth and add raw gluten pieces.
3. Cook gluten in broth, uncovered for 1 hour, boiling slowly.

APPENDIX A:

BIBLIOGRAPHY

1. Diet for a Small Planet
      by Frances Moore Lappe
      Ballentine Books - 1975

2. Diet for a New America
      by John Robins
      Stillpoint Publishing - 1987

3. The Vegetarian Alternative
      by Vic S. Sussman
      Rodale Press, Emmaus, Penn. 1978

4. Alive (The Canadian Journal of Health and Nutrition)
      Box 67333, Vancouver, B.C. V5W 3T1

5. Laurel's Kitchen
      by Laurel Robertson
      Bantam Books - 1976

6. The Chinese Vegetarian Cookbook
      by Gary Lee
      Nitty Gritty Prod., P.O. Box 5457,
      Concord, Cal., 94524

7. Natural Life Magazine
      Box 82447, Burnaby, B.C. V5C 5P8

8. Back to Eden
      by Jethro Kloss
      Woodbridge Press

9. Food for the Spirit (Vegetarianism in all the world religions)
      by Stephen Rosen
      Bala Books, Inc., 268 W. 23rd St., New York,
      NY 10011 1985

10. The Art of Indian Vegetarian Cooking
      by Yamuna Devi
      Bala Books, Inc., 268 W. 23rd St., New York,
      NY   10011 1985

11. The Higher Taste
      based on the teachings of His Divine Grace
      A.C. Bhaktivedanta Swami Prabhupada
      Bhaktivedanta Book Trust, 3764 Watseka Ave.,
      Los Angeles, Cal. 90034

136

APPENDIX B:
VITAMIN AND MINERAL CHART

VITAMIN A. Fat soluable; prevents night blindness and respiratory infections, needed for normal growth and teeth formation. Found in green and yellow vegetables, sprouts, apricots, pumpkins, dairy products.

VITAMIN B^1 (Thiamin). Can be destroyed by heat and is water soluable. Essential for normal functioning of nervous system and digestive tract. Very important for normal growth and proper use of starches and sugars. Promotes appetite. Deficiency may cause constipation, diarrhea, or beriberi. Found in vegetables (especially green, leafy ones), whole grains, legumes, wheat germ, brewers yeast, bananas, apples, dairy products, nuts, sprouts.

VITAMIN B^2 (Riboflavin). Heat stable but not light stable. Water soluable. Helps utilize food energy. Good for skin, eyes and digestive tract. Deficiency can cause weakness, headaches, and digestive trouble. Found in green, leafy vegetables, citrus fruits, tomatoes, dairy products, wheat germ, brewers yeast, legumes, whole grains, seeds, bananas.

VITAMIN B^3 (Niacin). Light and heat stable. Water soluable. Helps to utilize food energy. Good for the skin and digestive tract. Found in legumes, whole grains, leafy green vegetables dairy items, brewers yeast, wheat germ, tomatoes, peanuts.

VITAMIN B^{12}. Soluable in water or alcohol. Needed to form red blood cells and help prevent anemia. Found in brewers yeast (not all types), wheat germ, soybeans, peanuts.

VITAMIN C (Ascorbic Acid). Destroyed by heat or oxidation. Promotes healing and disease and infection resistance. Good for bones, teeth, and gums. Prevents scurvy. Lessens intensity of colds. Found in citrus fruits, tomatoes, potatoes, broccoli, cauliflower, strawberries. Most melons, fruits and vegetables have a little.

VITAMIN D. Some sources stable under refrigeration. Promotes calcium absorption. Good for normal growth of body formation of bones and teeth. Essential for children and pregnant women. Deficiency can cause ricketts and weakness. Found in sunlight, sunflower seeds, coconut, almonds, and dairy products, though not much unless they're enriched.

VITAMIN E. Heat stable and fat soluable. Improves oxygen efficiency of muscles. Good for reproduction system and heart. Good for burns and internal and external wounds. Good for pregnant women. Found in leafy green vegetables, natural oils, beets, nuts, seeds, oranges, molasses, legumes, peanuts.

MINERALS

CALCIUM. Good for bones and teeth. Helps regulate heartbeat and clot blood. Found in beet and turnip greens, lettuces, potatoes, dairy products, and almonds.

PHOSPHOROUS. Good for bones and teeth. Assists in waste removal and food absorption. Found in wheat, bran, wheat germ, skim milk powder, swiss cheese, cheddar cheese, yeast.

IRON. Helps form hemoglobin in red blood cells. Helps prevent anemia. Found in leafy green vegetables, dried fruit, molasses, legumes, whole grains.

IODINE. Regulates proper growth and development. Also regulates food use by the body. Found in kelp, dulse, seaweeds, iodized salt, leafy green vegetables.

MAGNESIUM. Relaxes nerves, helps digestion, also promotes new cell growth. Found in whole grains, eggplant, citrus fruits, coconuts.

POTASSIUM. Regulates weight, good for nerves and muscles. Found in molasses, dried fruits, whole grains, legumes, leafy green vegetables, nuts, bananas.

MANGANESE. Essential in forming blood cells, good for memory, good for pancreas. Found in buckwheat, whole grains, sunflower seeds, legumes, brewers yeast.

ZINC. Increases blood volume, promotes healing and proper growth. Found in brewers yeast, legumes, nuts and seeds.

INDEX

Diet for the 21st Century

OVEN TEMPERATURES

Below 300° F = very slow
300° F = slow
325° F = moderately slow
350° F = moderate
375° F = moderately hot
400°–425° F = hot
450°–475° F = very hot

Fahrenheit to Celsius (Centigrade):
Subtract 32 from Fahrenheit reading, multiply
by 5 then divide by 9.